Women in PR History

The history of PR has received limited attention over the years, and especially the role of women in PR has been an 'untold' story thus far. This book is the first attempt, following research presented at the International History of Public Relations Conference, to shed light on the significant role that female pioneers have played in the evolution of PR.

This book explores the field in a way that will offer insight of the significance that women had in the evolution of PR, with diverse chapters that provide rich perspectives on women's contributions to PR throughout the years and across the globe. It opens with an overview of women in public relations. Later chapters focus on the case of Turkey, which seems to have a rich history of women in public relations, then on specific cases from Oceania (Australia), Europe (Spain), Asia (Malaysia and Thailand) and America (United States). The final chapter deals with the case of Inez Kaiser, who was the first African-American women to open a US public relations agency.

This book will add knowledge and understanding to the fields of PR history and historiography. Academics and researchers will find the volume appropriate for research and teaching. Practitioners will also find the book extremely relevant for training, short courses and professional practice.

Anastasios Theofilou is Principal Academic in Public Relations at the Faculty of Media and Communication, at Bournemouth University, UK. He holds a BA in Political Science and Public Administration, specializing in International Relations, awarded by the University of Athens, an MBA awarded by the National Technical University of Athens and the Athens University of Economics and Business, and finally a PhD awarded by the Athens University of Economics and Business.

The History of Public Relations: A Global Approach
Series Editors

Dr Anastasios Theofilou
is Principal Academic in Public Relations in the Faculty of Media and Communication of Bournemouth University.

Professor Tom Watson, PhD,
is emeritus professor of Public Relations in the Faculty of Media and Communication of Bournemouth University.

The history of public relations (PR) has received limited attention over the years. Publications on the topic have been few and far between, while researchers and practitioners struggle to classify historical themes in PR. This series addresses that issue directly with the publication of eight separate books, each focusing on one of the most popular historical themes of PR as presented at the International History of Public Relations Conference (IHPRC). The project will make a major contribution to the history and historiography of PR, creating new knowledge and providing fresh perspectives to understanding the discipline. It will be the first to bring forward these different, sometimes alternative and culturally diverse, histories of public relations in a single format.

The History of Public Relations: A Global Approach series is for:

- researchers of marketing communications disciplines with a focus in communication, PR or political communication.
- advanced students of marketing communications disciplines with a major in communication or PR.
- academics in the field of communication who are interested in teaching or researching PR.
- practitioners wishing to understand the history of PR in order to enrich their practice of the discipline.

Women in PR History
Edited by Anastasios Theofilou

For more information about this series, please visit: www.routledge.com/series/HPR.

Women in PR History

Edited by
Anastasios Theofilou

LONDON AND NEW YORK

First published 2021
by Routledge
2 Park Square, Milton Park, Abingdon, Oxon OX14 4RN

and by Routledge
52 Vanderbilt Avenue, New York, NY 10017

Routledge is an imprint of the Taylor & Francis Group, an informa business

© 2021 selection and editorial matter, Anastasios Theofilou; individual chapters, the contributors

The right of Anastasios Theofilou to be identified as the author of the editorial material, and of the authors for their individual chapters, has been asserted in accordance with sections 77 and 78 of the Copyright, Designs and Patents Act 1988.

All rights reserved. No part of this book may be reprinted or reproduced or utilised in any form or by any electronic, mechanical, or other means, now known or hereafter invented, including photocopying and recording, or in any information storage or retrieval system, without permission in writing from the publishers.

Trademark notice: Product or corporate names may be trademarks or registered trademarks, and are used only for identification and explanation without intent to infringe.

British Library Cataloguing-in-Publication Data
A catalogue record for this book is available from the British Library

Library of Congress Cataloging-in-Publication Data
Names: Theofilou, Anastasios, editor.
Title: Women in PR history / edited by Anastasios Theofilou.
Description: Abingdon, Oxford ; New York, NY : Routledge, 2021. |
Series: The history of public relations: a global approach |
Includes bibliographical references and index.
Identifiers: LCCN 2020036217 (print) | LCCN 2020036218 (ebook)
Subjects: LCSH: Public relations–History. | Women public relations personnel–History. Classification: LCC HD59 .W558 2021 (print) |
LCC HD59 (ebook) | DDC 659.2082–dc23
LC record available at https://lccn.loc.gov/2020036217
LC ebook record available at https://lccn.loc.gov/2020036218

ISBN: 978-0-367-47659-5 (hbk)
ISBN: 978-1-003-03571-8 (ebk)

Typeset in ITC Galliard Std
by Newgen Publishing UK

Contents

List of contributors vii

Introduction 1
ANASTASIOS THEOFILOU

1 Re-examining the existence of the "velvet ghetto" and the "glass ceiling": examining the status of American women in public relations a generation later 9
DONALD K. WRIGHT

2 Women in public relations: a thematic analysis of ECM data (2009–2019) 18
MARTINA TOPIĆ AND RALPH TENCH

3 'Signum authenticum' of women: herstories in Turkey's public relations during the early years 31
MELIKE AKTAŞ, G. SENEM GENÇTÜRK HIZAL AND B. PINAR ÖZDEMIR

4 Professional standards of PR in three decades through the lenses of Turkish women presidents of IPRA 41
PELIN HÜRMERIÇ AND A. BANU BIÇAKÇI

5 Betty Stewart, Orientalism and *Oriental Cavalcade*: entertainment public relations in late 1950s Australia 57
KATE FITCH

6 The militant documentary films of Helena Lumbreras as dissent and protest public relations 67
ISADORA GUARDIA, CAROLINA MARTÍNEZ AND JORDI XIFRA

7 A 'herstory' of Malaysian public relations: Paddy Schubert, Malaysia's women PR pioneer 80
RIZWANAH SOUKET

8 The Loi Krathong festival and Nang Noppamas: Applying current 'PR' theory to identify the first Thai female PR practitioner 91
PARICHART STHAPITANONDA

9 Inez Kaiser: the perseverance of a public relations pioneer 104
DENISE HILL AND SHELLEY SPECTOR

Conclusions 116
ANASTASIOS THEOFILOU

Index 118

Contributors

Melike Aktaş is an associate professor in Ankara University Faculty of Communication, Public Relations and Publicity Department. Her research interests include consumer studies, consumption relationships, public relations theory, public relations researches and public relations history. She is one of the co-authors of the book titled as *Türkiye'de Halkla İlişkiler Tarihi: Kurumsallaşma Yılları 1960–1980* [Public Relations History in Turkey: Institutionalization Years 1960–1980].

A. Banu Bıçakçı (PhD) is an associate professor of Public Relations. Currently she is a part-time lecturer at İzmir University of Economics and a communication consultant for the Association of Organic Agriculture Associations (ETO *Derneği*). Her research interests primarily involve PR history, sustainability and activist public relations. She has been conducting research in EUPRERA PR History network for seven years, and she is a member of EUPRERA, ECREA and IAMCR.

Kate Fitch is a senior lecturer in Communication and Media Studies in the School of Media, Film and Journalism at Monash University in Melbourne, Australia, where she coordinates the public relations specialisation. She previously worked at Murdoch University, where she founded the public relations major and chaired the programme for ten years. Her book, *Professionalizing Public Relations: History, Gender and Education*, offered the first sociological history of Australian public relations in the twentieth century and her forthcoming book, co-authored with Professor Judy Motion, *Popular Culture and Social Change: The Hidden Work of Public Relations*, investigates the impact of public relations on contemporary culture. Her research interests and publications span critical public relations perspectives on gender, history and promotional culture.

Isadora Guardia is a documentary film-maker and associate professor at the Valencia University. Her research focuses basically on the relationship between political documentary and social reality, being an expert in Spanish militant cinema and in the figure of the film-maker Helena Lumbreras. She has published numerous articles on documentary film and social intervention.

Denise Hill (PhD, APR) is an associate professor at Elon University's School of Communications, where she teaches undergraduate and graduate courses in strategic communications. She is a former chief communications officer with more than 30 years of corporate communications and public relations agency experience. Hill holds a bachelor's degree and master's degree in communications from Temple University and a PhD in mass communication from the University of North Carolina at Chapel Hill. She is on the board of directors of the Public Relations Society of America, the advisory board of the Museum of Public Relations, and is a member of the Arthur W. Page Society, the Association for Education in Journalism and Mass Communication, and the American Journalism Historians Association.

G. Senem Gençtürk Hızal is working as a professor in the Department of Public Relations and Publicity at Başkent University. Her research interests lie in the area of advertising, public relations and media industry within the context of history. She is one of the co-authors of the book titled as *Türkiye'de Halkla İlişkiler Tarihi: Kurumsallaşma Yılları 1960–1980* [Public Relations History in Turkey: Institutionalization Years 1960–1980].

Pelin Hürmeriç (PhD) is an associate professor of Public Relations. She is the vice dean of the Faculty of Communication and Chair of the Department of Public Relations and Publicity at Yeditepe University, İstanbul, where she has been a faculty member since 2001. Her research interests are in the fields of PR history and corporate communications. She is a member of EUPRERA, ECREA and IAMCR.

Carolina Martínez is associate professor and researcher in Theatre and Cinema Studies at the Girona University (ERAM) and a member of Valladolid International Film Festival Selection Committee. She has published a wide range of papers and book chapters on experimental and documentary cinema, videodance and performing arts, as well as edited an anthology of texts of the avant-garde film-maker Maya Deren. She has also enjoyed an extensive career as cinema administrator and as theatre performer.

B. Pınar Özdemir is an associate professor at Ankara University, Faculty of Communication, Department of Public Relations and Publicity. Her major research areas are public relations history, non-profit public relations and digital public relations. She has several published articles, book chapters and books. She is one of the co-authors of the book titled as *Türkiye'de Halkla İlişkiler Tarihi: Kurumsallaşma Yılları 1960–1980* [Public Relations History in Turkey: Institutionalization Years 1960–1980].

Rizwanah Souket is a lecturer in public relations at the School of Arts, Monash University Malaysia. Her doctoral research traces the public relations lineage in Malaysia and provides a concrete documented history of Malaysian public relations. Her research interests include public relations, history and historiography, gender role, voter behaviour, political communication, and media effects. Dr. Rizwanah is also an active member of the Malaysian Institute of Public Relations (IPRM) and of the Public Relations & Communications Association (PRCA) Southeast Asia.

Shelley Spector is the founder and director of the Museum of Public Relations, the world's only educational institution dedicated to collecting, preserving and documenting the industry's history. She is also the founder and president of Spector and Associates, Inc., a New York-based public relations agency. She is also on the faculty of the Public Relations/Corporate Communications M.A. programme at New York University.

Spector holds a bachelor's degree in Journalism from the University of Rhode Island and a master's degree in TV/Radio and Film from the Newhouse School at Syracuse University.

She serves on the steering committee of the Diversity Action Alliance and the diversity committees of the Arthur W. Page Society and the PR Council.

Parichart Sthapitanonda is a professor and a former dean of the faculty of Communication Arts, Chulalongkorn University. She also serves as the independent director of MCOT Public Co. Ltd., and Thailand Post Col. Ltd. She received an undergraduate degree and a graduate degree from Chulalongkorn University in Thailand and a doctoral degree from Ohio University. Her area of interest includes public relations, communication campaign management, CSR communication and sustainability

Anastasios Theofilou is Principal Academic in Public Relations at the Faculty of Media and Communication, at Bournemouth University, UK. He holds a BA in Political Science and Public Administration, specializing in International Relations awarded by the University of Athens, an MBA awarded by the National Technical University of Athens and the Athens University of Economics & Business, and finally a PhD awarded by the Athens University of Business and Economics. Anastasios' research interests expand on all aspects of organizational communication including crisis management, CSR, sponsorship and history of public relations. He has held various roles such as (amongst others) Head of Department, chief examiner for the Charted Institute of Public Relations (CIPR) and chair of the IHPRC.

Martina Topić is a senior lecturer in Public Relations in Leeds Business School. She was project lead for the British Academy funded project on Women in UK's Advertising Industry and Higher Education Funding Council for England (HEFCE-funded project on Women in British Journalism). She currently leads EUPRERA project on women in public relations, HEFCE funded projects on Women in PR and Marketing and HEFCE funded project on research-based teaching.

She is a member of the editorial board of several academic journals including Sociology (British Sociological Association) and The Qualitative Report (Nova Southeastern University). She is an editor of the section 'Culture, Media and

Film' of *Cogent Arts and Humanities* open-access journal (Taylor and Francis). More about her work can be found here: https://martinatopic.com/.

Ralph Tench is director of Research for Leeds Business School and President (2017–2020) European Public Relations Research and Education Association. Tench's research involves national and international projects. Professor Tench has written and edited 26 books; published over 40 academic journal papers; presented worldwide 60+ peer-reviewed reviewed papers. Books include the market leading strategic communication textbook, *Exploring Public Relations*, and recently *Communication Excellence: How to Develop, Manage and Lead Exceptional Communications*, based on the longitudinal, annual European Communication Monitor project (14 years, www.communicationmontor.eu). Tench's research focuses on strategic communication and its impact on societal issues including health, business, social and public policy.

Donald K. Wright (PhD) is chair of the Department of Mass Communication, Advertising & Public Relations and the Harold Burson Professor of Public Relations in the Boston University College of Communication. PRWeek magazine has recognized him both as one of the top 10 public relations educators in the United States and as one of the '15 Leading Lights' in US public relations. He is a long-time member of the Board of Trustees of the Institute for Public Relations (IPR) and served as a member of the Board of Trustees of the Arthur W. Page Society for 24 years. He is a past president of the International Public Relations Association (IPRA) and was the founding editor-in-chief of PRSA's *Public Relations Journal*, the world's first quarterly, open-access peer-reviewed electronic research journal in public relations. Professor Wright is an active consultant in public opinion research, employee communications, organizational ethics, professional development as well as management and structure of the corporate communications function.

Jordi Xifra is a professor at the Pompeu Fabra University, Barcelona. His research focuses basically on intellectual history of public relations, as well as the relationship between public relations and film studies. He has published more than 15 books on public relations and public affairs in Spain and South America, and his articles have been accepted for publication in *Public Relations Review*, *Journal of Public Relations Research* and *American Behavioural Scientist*, among others.

Introduction

Anastasios Theofilou

The role of women in PR has been an 'untold' story thus far. This book is the first attempt, following research presented at the International History of Public Relations Conference (IHPRC), to shed light on the topic. The book opens with the first two chapters providing an overview of women in public relations.

According to Donald Wright, the public relations industry has been concerned with matters of gender diversity for decades. Much of this interest in the United States began more than a quarter century ago when the foundations of two of the world's largest and most successful professional societies commissioned major research studies on the subject. One of these was funded by the International Association of Business Communicators (IABC) Foundation and became known as the 'Velvet Ghetto' Report – Cline, Masel-Walters, Toth, Turk, Smith & Johnson (1986). Meanwhile, the other was supported by the PRSA Foundation and was referred to frequently as the 'Glass Ceiling' Report – Wright, Grunig, Springston & Toth (1991). These major studies, plus research conducted by Theus (1985), Broom & Dozier (1986), Grunig (1988), Dozier (1988), Creedon (1991), Hon, Grunig & Dozier (1992), Toth & Grunig (1993) and Wrigley (2002), formed the basis of a considerable amount of research studying gender issues in United States public relations during the 1980s and 1990s. This gender research shed light on a number of concerns that were being faced at that time by women in the public relations industry, particularly citing three major areas. They were salary discrepancies between men and women, differences between the specific kinds of public relations work men and women were being asked to perform – with more women functioning in communication technician roles and more men performing as managers and executives – and concerns that men held an unusually high percentage of the truly senior-level positions in American public relations. The paper proposed for the IHPRC 2016 thoroughly reviewed gender research studies of American public relations in the 1980s and 1990s and then reported on the current status, examining gender inequities in American public relations based upon salary, division of work and the percentage of women now holding senior-level positions. During much of the 1980s and 1990s, data indicated the gender ratio of those practicing public relations in the United States was approximately 55:45 in favour of men. According to PR Week, the US gender ratio in 2015 had changed to become 70:30 in favour of women.

With more women working in the field today, it will be interesting to see if this has impacted gender equity in public relations particularly in terms of salaries, role responsibilities and senior-level employment status. Salary differences will be measured via interviews with representatives of three major recruiting companies; role responsibilities will be gauged through interviews with some of the leading female public relations managers; and senior-level status will be examined based upon membership rosters of organizations, such as the (PR) Seminar and the Arthur W. Page Society.

In the next chapter, Martina Topić and Ralph Tench look at findings from the European Communications Monitor (ECM) in the period from 2009 to 2019. In the decade that ECM covered, women in public relations reported several issues; for example, in early periods of research, they were reporting glass ceiling and the pay gap. However, as the ECM research progressed, women started to report other issues, such as lack of mentoring opportunities and better job security for men, low influence in the department and having fewer skills in online developments, such as visual communication and video editing. This is once more linked to the dominance of men in higher positions and the fact men report in ECM surveys good relationships with senior management, while women report better relationships with external stakeholders and clients. In the last three years, increased workloads and the precariousness of job roles have led women to report higher stress levels than men and lower job satisfaction. Thus, Topić and Tench demonstrate that women continually face precarious work situations and a lack of equal opportunities. While PR is a feminized industry and women have progressed to mid-level management, they still struggle to obtain senior positions, and, nevertheless, the lack of resources seems to be hitting women's line of management more, thus causing stress and job dissatisfaction.

Chapters 4 and 5 focus on the case of Turkey, which seems to have a rich history of women in public relations. Women have shaped the discipline nationally and through their work with the International Public Relations Associations (IPRA).

Based on Melike Aktaş, Pınar Özdemir and Senem Gençtürk Hızal, women had major roles and significant influences on the establishment and development of the public relations field in Turkey. Starting from the mid-1950s, several women from academia and the private and public sectors have shaped this new profession and discipline through their knowledge, skills and practices. Women pioneers established the first PR agency and ran the first in-house PR departments, both in private and public institutions. Furthermore, the first president and several board members were women when the Public Relations Association of Turkey was established in 1972. In addition, the field in Turkey was entitled by a pioneer woman academic who also translated the first academic texts and took part in the development of PR education. During the institutionalization years of Turkish public relations (1960–1980), influential women practitioners worked as editors of employee publications, as account supervisors, as event managers and as media spokespeople. Although female contributions to the field were remarkable, the stories of these women were mostly unheard, unseen and under-researched in

Turkey. Based on an oral history research, this paper aims to present stories of women pioneers through highlighting their contributions to the development of the field. In-depth interviews were conducted with Nermin Abadan Unat, Canan Usman Reeves, Ayşegül Dora, Betûl Mardin, Birten Gökyay and Birkan Uysal to harvest their experiences, achievements, difficulties and frustrations. Women pioneers' commonalities, in terms of social networks, social origin and cultural/economic capital, are also discussed in order to uncover the pattern of professional development of public relations in Turkey.

Pelin Hürmeriç and A. Banu Bıçakçı highlight the role of women in the IPRA. In public relations literature, a number of researches aim to analyse the role and impact of women in the public relations profession (Broom, 1982; Toth & Grunig, 1993; Krider & Ross, 1997; Wrigley, 2002; Siler, 2009; Creedon, 2011; Tsetsura, 2011; Place, 2012; Yaxley, 2013; Bıçakçı & Hürmeriç, 2013; Öksüz & Görpe, 2014). However, those studies often focus on the gender roles and challenges that women PR practitioners face all around the world. Regarding the Associations' point of view, although there are two studies related with the women in the International Association of Business Communicators (IABC, 1986 and updated in 2003), there is only one study (McDonald, 2009) that focuses on women in a PR association (PRSA – Public Relations Society of America). One of the most reputable associations regarding the public relations profession is IPRA, founded in London, 1955 (https://microsites.bournemouth.ac.uk/historyofpr/files/2011/11/IPRA-ARCHIVE-May-2015.pdf), with the aim of raising the standards of PR practice worldwide. The Association has had a number of woman presidents in its 60-year history. In 1995, Betûl Mardin, already the first woman public relations practitioner in Turkey, became the first Turkish and Muslim president of IPRA, raising Turkey's profile within the public relations profession and increasing international co-operation in various PR projects (Bıçakçı & Hürmeriç, 2014, p. 263). Ceyda Aydede, who was the president of a PR agency named 'Global PR Agency', became the second Turkish IPRA president in 2003 (Bıçakçı & Hürmeriç, 2013, p. 98). In 2014, the founder and president of the 'Stage PR Agency', Zehra Güngör, became the third Turkish and 50th IPRA president. The main aim of this study is to shed light on the role of these three women presidents of IPRA in terms of the development of the public relations profession. The study will contribute to the body of knowledge in the PR profession by examining the three decades of the IPRA (1990s, 2000s and 2010s) that were managed by the three Turkish women presidents. In order to reveal their professional stories ('her-story'), the primary research is based on the in-depth interviews conducted with Betûl Mardin, Ceyda Aydede and Zehra Güngör. IPRA archives (presidents' personal archives and IPRA archive in Bournemouth University) will also be analysed in order to reveal related data.

The following chapters focus on specific cases from Oceania (Australia), Europe (Spain), Asia (Malaysia and Thailand) and America (United States).

Kate Fitch's chapter offers important insights into Australian public relations history. Researching forgotten campaigns, such as Betty Stewart's work on *Oriental Cavalcade* in 1959, it highlights the ways Australian public relations history is gendered and illuminates the work done in understudied sectors, such as entertainment public relations. The research presented in this chapter therefore offers an opportunity for rethinking public relations practices and history beyond corporate parameters and gendered professional histories. Promoting *Oriental Cavalcade* as the mysterious East and highlighting the 'beautiful' Japanese dance troupe drew on many Asian tropes. The commodification of entertainers as 'exotic Asians' was primarily the public relations strategy underpinning the *Oriental Cavalcade* campaign, which relied heavily on media relations and cross-promotion with media and charity sectors. Stewart deliberately sought to contrast Australia-Asia cultures, evident in the staged photo opportunities with kimonos and rickshaws for the press. Stewart's first campaign as a consultant coincides with the decade the industry sought professional legitimacy, with the founding of state-based professional institutes and public relations consultancies. The fact that Stewart's decision to open a public relations consultancy is largely unheralded points to the urgent need for more 'herstories' in order to more fully comprehend the historical development of public relations in Australia.

Isadora Guardia, Carolina Martínez and Jordi Xifra examine the case of Helen Lumbreras. Helena Lumbreras (deceased in 1995) represents one of the major players in the anti-Franco militant cinema in the 1960s and 1970s. She began her career in Italy as a director and scriptwriter of documentaries for RAI. Afterwards, she assumed the role of assistant director to Fellini, Rosi, Pontecorvo and Pasolini. She signed an agreement with Unicité (a production company close to the Italian Communist Party) to shoot a medium length film in Spain about the anti-Franco movement. Returning to Spain in 1968, she made political and activist documentaries. All those films were made from the secrecy. She co-founded Colectivo de Cine de Clase (Film of Class Group), whose main objective was 'to film dreams of people who were struggling to improve their living conditions'. Later, she contacted filmmaker Llorenç Soler in Barcelona, and, in 1970, she shot the documentary *El Cuarto Poder* (The Fourth Power), a lucid analysis of the main Spanish newspapers (both legal and illegal) at that time. In August 1971, Lumbreras was arrested by the police and consequently dismissed from her work, as well as being expelled from the Communist Party. Under this context, the first film emerged of Colectivo de Cine de Clase, El campo para el hombre (The field for men, 1975), which was filmed in various rural areas of Galicia and Andalusia, providing the peasants and labourers with an opportunity to express their wishes and claims openly. After the death of Franco, news coming from Spain was highly valued by international TV channels, and a minute could be sold for a thousand dollars. Thanks to that, Colectivo de Cine de Clase had enough income to fund two projects. Firstly, *O todos o ninguno* (Or all or none, 1976) is a documentary about the struggle of workers in a metalworking firm in Cornellá ('an Andalusian town in Catalonia', Lumbreras said). The second is titled *A la vuelta del grito* (After the cry, 1978) and is a film made with more funds and directed with formal experimentation. In 1978, coinciding with the start of dismantling of the basic labour movement that occurred in the early years of the transition, the group disbanded. The case of Lumbreras is a good example of activism from the margins; using documentary discourse, Lumbreras claimed social change. Helena Lumbreras is an example of the inter-relationships of public relations and social change, and, from this perspective, Lumbreras played an important role in the Spanish hidden history of public relations.

Rizwanah Souket sheds light on one phenomenal woman who has contributed immensely to Malaysian public relations as a prolific writer, activist, counsel and pioneer educationist. This chapter documents a 'her-story' of Paddy Schubert (now called Paddy Bowie) and her 60 years of experience in Malaysian public relations. Paddy Schubert, a British-born Malaysian, is a public relations pioneer in her own right. Graduating from Manchester University and Oxford University, she began her career as a teacher. In 1960, she joined Shell Malaysia and during a period when women's work was marginalized, she became the first woman to take on the role of the Trade Relations Director in the Shell Group of companies and was responsible for the firm's public relations. The Institute of Public Relations Malaysia (IPRM), formed in 1961, advocated for education and training in order to enhance the standard and jurisdiction of public relations in Malaysia (Idid, 2005). Paddy Schubert was appointed as one of the directors to run the Institute's first certificate course, introduced in 1971, thus making her the first woman PR educationist in Malaysia. Under her tenure, more than half of the participants passing the course were women. In 1980, Schubert started her own PR consultancy called Paddy Schubert Consultants Sdn Bhd, a business and consultancy group that she still chairs at 95 years old. Paddy Schubert advocated for women issues, such as women's position in the Malaysian work force, working closely with leaders, such as Mahathir, the current Prime Minister of Malaysia. In 2007, she received the Order of the British Empire (OBE) for her role in establishing cordial links between UK and Malaysia. Her endeavours and accomplishments are chronicled in her book, *Paddy: A Lifetime of Memories* (Schubert 2018). This research incorporates a historical approach based on primary sources in the form of personal interviews, newspaper archives and private materials in the form of books written by Paddy Schubert. The resultant story is organized chronologically and presented as a tale of Malaysian public relations. It offers unique insights into Schubert's contributions to the professionalization of public relations in Malaysia over six decades.

Parichart Sthapitanonda explores whether or not Ms. Noppamas should be recognized as the first female PR person in Thai history. The 'Loi Krathong' Festival is one of the most celebrated events in Thailand. Every year, all rivers, canals and ponds in Thailand are illuminated with millions of candle-lit 'Krathongs' at night time. The word 'Krathong' means a small floating vessel with the lotus style. These vessels are made from natural banana leaves and decorated with incenses, candles and flowers. At the international level, the Thai Government and the Tourism Authority of Thailand (TAT) have joined private and public partners to highlight the 'Loi Krathog' Festival worldwide as a part of promoting the travel industry in Thailand for decades. Significantly, this special event is recognized in all kinds of Thai public relations tools used for Thai tourism promotion. The major focus of the event is an image of a beautiful Thai woman with a friendly smile, who is always dressed in a local Thai traditional style with a 'Krathong' in her hand. Otherwise, they show her taking a lotus-style Krathong to the river and letting it go (known as 'Loi' in Thai). Local Thai citizens, of all ages and from all walks of life, highly recognize this woman as Ms. Noppamas. The objective of this article is to focus on Ms. Noppamas from a public relations perspective. Based on the documentary analysis of her life in Thai history, this paper claims that she was the first Thai woman to play the role of what we currently recognize as a PR person. Turning back to the history of Thailand, this paper seeks to find evidences to claim that Ms. Noppamas dedicated herself to ancient Thai PR activities. By looking to the past, Ms. Noppamas was claimed as one of the Thai women in history when the first Thai kingdom was found. She was an ordinary woman playing a significant role because people believed she 'created' Krathong from banana leaves in a unique lotus-shaped style and used it as a floating vessel to pay respect to the mother of the rivers. According to Thai oral history, the King appreciated her creativity and decided to make a formal announcement to use Noppamas' original version of vessels as the symbol of the 'Loi Krathong' festival. Some stories claimed that the king promoted her as his most 'favourite' consort during the old days. Some documents mentioned that she was later promoted to have a higher rank as a senior official called 'Tao Sri Chulalak' since she was the first lady to write a book to women on how to behave officially if they want to compete with men and be selected as a civil servant. However, her story is currently arguable. On one hand, contemporary historians tried to discredit 'her story' and claimed that she did not exist in early history and it was less possible to celebrate 'Loi Kratong' Festival since the water was insufficient in that old capital city. They tried to show that the King wrote up her story as a propaganda tool for visualizing the 'ideal' picture of the old days and the 'ideal' woman from the male perspective. On the other hand, others presented the defence that she existed in the 'real' oral history. However, the local people failed to save the old handwritten documents of past ages due to wars, fires or the way these notes were taken. They claimed that King Rama IV wrote up her story based on an oral history and formally shared it with the public after modern publishing machines were introduced in Thailand some hundred years ago. To conclude, no matter who she is, or whether she was in Thai history or not, Thai people perceive her as a traditional role model, who promotes Thai female characteristics, the Thai way of smiling and Thai way of dressing and created the first PR event for recognizing the value of water as 'Loi Krathong'. Her story is widespread, from Word of Mouth to published documents and promotional materials. Additionally, a number of Thai women have entered competitions to be selected as 'Ms. Noppamas' of the 'Loi Kratong' Festival.

Finally, Denise Hill and Shelley Spector deal with the case of Inez Kaiser. Inez Kaiser was the first African-American women to open a US public relations agency, one that served national accounts like Lever Brothers, Sears and 7Up. She started her agency in 1957, a year in which a number of pivotal events took place that helped augur the modern US civil rights movement. That timeframe was also one in which national consumer brands were beginning to recognize the previously ignored growing African-American marketplace. Kaiser capitalized on this growth and positioned her firm as one uniquely qualified to reach the black consumer. Even with her experience, she faced obstacles, not just as a woman but as a black woman, operating her business in the racially segregated American Midwest. Regardless of the challenges she faced, Kaiser persevered and ran her agency for more than 50 years. Despite the recognition she achieved for her civic work, Kaiser, who died in 2016 aged 98, has never been fully recognized as a public relations pioneer. When she has been acknowledged, her work has been relegated to a paragraph in the public relations history section of some textbooks. This chapter goes beyond that one paragraph and provides the first published overview of Kaiser's life and work.

This book finishes with a chapter summarizing the concluding remarks from all outputs presented. I sincerely hope that the readers find this book as inspirational and enjoyable as I found editing it.

References

Association for Education in Journalism (1980). *A Comparison of Roles Played by Men and Women in Public Relations*, Boston: Broom, G. M.

Bıçakçı, A. B., & Hürmeriç, P. (2013). Milestones in Turkish public relations history, *Public Relations Review*, 39(2), 91–100.

Bıçakçı, A. B., & Hürmeriç, P. (2014). The historical development of public relations profession in Turkey: The rise of a profession in times of social transformation, In Burton St. J. III, Lamme M. O., L'Etang J. (Eds.). *Pathways to Public Relations: Histories of Practice and Profession*, London: Routledge.

Cline, C. G., Masel-Walters, L., Toth, E. L., Turk, J. V., Smith, H. T., & Johnson, N. (1986). *The Velvet Ghetto: The Impact of the Increasing Percentage of Women in Public Relations and Organizational Communication*. San Francisco: IABC Foundation.

Creedon, P. L. (1991). Public relations and women's work: Toward a feminist analysis of public relations roles, *Public Relations Research Annual*, 3, 67–84.

Creedon, P. J. (2011). Public relations and "Women's Work": Toward a feminist analysis of public relations roles. In Grunig, L. A & Grunig, J. E., (Eds.). *Public Relations Research Annual*. London, Routledge.

Broom, G. M. (1982). A comparison of sex roles in public relations, *Public Relations Review*, 8 (3), 17–22.

Broom, G. M., & Dozier, D. M. (1986). Advancement for public relations role models. *Public Relations Review*, 12(1), 37–56.

Dozier, D. M. (1988). Breaking public relations' glass ceiling, *Public Relations Review*, 14(3), 6–14.

Fidelzeid, G. (2015, March 2). How to close the gender pay gap in PR. PR Week. www.prweek.com/article/1335944/close-gender-pay-gap-pr. Accessed July 22, 2015.

Grunig, L. A. (1988). A research agenda for women in public relations, *Public Relations Review*, 14(3), 18–57.

Hon, L. C., Grunig, L. A., & Dozier, D. M. (1992). Women in public relations: Problems and opportunities, 419–438. In Grunig, J. E. (Ed.), *Excellence in Public Relations and Communication Management*. Hillsdale, NJ: Lawrence Erlbaum.

Idid, S. A. (2005). *Institute of Public Relations Malaysia*. Kuala Lumpur, Malaysia: International Islamic University Malaysia, pp. 71–80.

Krider, D. S., & Ross, P. G. (1997). The experiences of women in a public relations firm: A phenomenological explication, *Journal of Business Communication*, 34(4), 437–454.

Öksüz, B., & Görpe, S. (2014). Woman's place in the field of public relations in Turkey: Perspectives of academics, practitioners, and representatives of professional organizations on it, İstanbul Üniversitesi İletişim Fakültesi Dergisi, *Journal of İstanbul University, Faculty of Communication*, 2(47), 125–142.

Place, K. R. (2012). Power-control or empowerment? How women public relations practitioners make meaning of power, *Journal of Public Relations Research*, 24, 435–450.

Schubert, P. (2018). *Paddy, A Lifetime of Memories*. Kuala Lumpur: Paddy Schubert Consultants Sdn Bhd

Sha, A. (2015). "Why aren't there more female CEOs in PR"? Holmes Report. (April). Accessed at: www.holmesreport.com/long-reads/article/why-aren't-there-more-female-ceos-in-pr.

Siler, M. N. (2009). *Telling the Story of Women's Contributions to Public Relations: A Content Analysis of Three Public Relations Industry Publications*, 2001–2005. (Unpublished MA dissertation). Ball State University, Indiana.

Taff, H. P. (2003, February–March). Times Have Changed? IABC Research Foundation's 'The Velvet Ghetto' Study Revisited, Communication World, 10–11.

Theus, K. T. (1985). Gender shifts in journalism and public relations, *Public Relations Review*, 11(1), 42–50.

Toth, E. L., & Grunig, L. A. (1993). The missing story of women in public relations, *Journal of Public Relations Research*, 5(3), 153–175.

Tsetsura, K. (2011). Is public relations a real job? How female practitioners construct the profession, *Journal of Public Relations Research*, 23(1), 1–23.

Wright, D. K., Grunig, L. A., Springston, J. K., & Toth, E. L. (1991). Under the glass ceiling: An analysis of gender issues in American public relations. New York: Public Relations Society of America Foundation Monograph Series, 1(2).

Wrigley, B. J. (2002). Glass ceiling? What glass ceiling? A qualitative study of how women view the glass ceiling in public relations and communications management, *Journal of Public Relations Research*, 14(1), 27–55.

Yaxley, H. M. L. (2013). Career experiences of women in British public relations, *Public Relations Review*, 39, 156–165.

1 Re-examining the existence of the "velvet ghetto" and the "glass ceiling"

Examining the status of American women in public relations a generation later

Donald K. Wright

Introduction

The public relations (PR) industry has been concerned with matters of gender diversity for decades. In the United States, much of this interest began more than 40 years ago when the foundations of two of the world's largest and most successful professional societies commissioned major research studies on the subject.

One of these was funded by the International Association of Business Communicators (IABC) Foundation and became known as the "velvet ghetto" report (Cline, Masel-Walters, Toth, Turk, Smith & Johnson, 1986), while the other was supported by the Public Relations Society of America (PRSA) Foundation and was referred to frequently as the "glass ceiling" report (Wright, L. Grunig, Springston & Toth, 1991). These major studies, plus research conducted by Theus (1985), Broom & Dozier (1986), L. Grunig (1988), Dozier (1988), Creedon (1991), Hon, L. Grunig & Dozier (1992), Toth & Grunig (1993) and Wrigley (2002), formed the basis of a considerable amount of research studying gender issues in the United States public relations during the 1980s and 1990s.

These works stimulated all sorts of discussion and additional research about gender and public relations practice, including concerns from one noted practitioner that women were in the process of inheriting the profession (Bates, 1983) and a series of other thoughts suggesting the public relations industry was being "hurt" by having too many women practitioners (Bernstein, 1987).

This gender research shed light on a number of concerns being faced at that time by women in the public relations industry; particularly, three major areas were cited. They were salary discrepancies between men and women, differences between the specific kinds of public relations work men and women were being asked to perform – more women functioning in communication technician roles and more men performing as communication managers and executives – and concerns that men held an unusually high percentage of the truly senior-level positions in American public relations.

The purpose of this chapter is to review gender research studies about American public relations in the 1980s and 1990s and then report on the current status, examining gender inequities in American public relations based upon salary, division of work, and the percentage of women now holding senior-level positions.

During much of the 1980s and 1990s, data indicated about 55 percent of those practicing public relations in the United States were male and about 45 percent were female. According to *PR Week*, the US gender division in 2015 was 70 percent female and 30 percent male.

Literature review

According to Toth (1988), the IABC "velvet ghetto" study worked off three assumptions. Firstly, women working in the public relations industry were more likely than men to perceive themselves as "technicians" rather than as "managers." Secondly, even when other variables were controlled and both men and women were performing similar public relations work, women were paid substantially less than men. Thirdly, female-dominated occupations have diminished salary and status when compared with male-dominated occupational groups. Other public relations scholars of the same era reported similar findings (Wright et al. 1991, Theus, 1985; Broom & Dozier, 1986; L. Grunig, 1988; Dozier, 1988; Hon, L. Grunig & Dozier, 1992; Toth & L. Gruinig, 1993; Wrigley, 2002).

Reporting on the IABC "velvet ghetto" study's results, particularly on the differences between female-dominated and male-dominated industries, Taff (2003) found little overt management and salary bias against women working in public relations but did report the existence of significant gender-based salary gaps. This study also found a "socialization process" was working against women, resulting in many self-selecting into technician (as opposed to managerial) occupational roles. Two noted public relations educators reported similar findings in a research project exploring the "velvet ghetto" in PR education (Zoch & Russell, 1991).

Work–life balance

More recent research emphasizing gender and public relations has focused on the topic of work–life-balance. A study by Aldoory et al. (2008) found both men and women generally believe balancing work and family is a "woman's issue." This research also found some of the female focus group participants (but none of the male respondents) blamed women for "making it harder on women." Some of the women in this study apparently resigned themselves to the belief there was no such thing as a work–life balance. Additionally, both male and female participants in this study mentioned a perceived need to enact masculine career qualities, while both expressed the need for women to be more responsive to motherhood and civic engagement.

Salary differences

According to Taff (2003), women in the US national workforce were paid 73 cents for every one dollar paid to a male counterpart in 2000. These financial inequities most certainly appear to have been carried over into public relations practice. As Hon (1992) and others have pointed out, career-long salary differences between men and women working in public relations can surpass $US 1 million. Toth & Cline (1989) reported the existence of what they called "unmitigated gender differences in median and mean salaries" between men and women working in the public relations industry.

Scholarship suggests the barriers faced by women run considerably deeper than financial ones (Hon et al., 1992). Dozier, Sha & Shen (2013) report that US households headed by women are significantly more likely than other kinds of households to be living below the federal poverty level. They also suggest the gender pay gap in public relations is impacted by other factors, including women having less professional experience than men, women tending to function in communication technician roles vis-à-vis male-dominated managerial communication roles and women being much less active than men in organizational decision-making, which is significantly related to income.

Women in public relations leadership

Another important historical difference between women and men working in public relations involves the reality men are more likely than women to serve in positions of organizational leadership; however, this might be changing. Based on membership in the Arthur W. Page Society (an organization advancing the executive role of corporate public relations managers), women appear to be moving into public relations executive positions at a faster pace than men. In 1991, only six percent of Page's members were women, but that important statistic had grown to 44 percent by 2015. However, as reported in *PRWeek*, women continue to be paid less than men, especially at the executive level.

Other factors

Most of the early academic scholarship studying gender in American public relations was based upon surveys and interviews with members of the IABC and/or the PRSA. Both of these professional associations have membership numbers of about 22,500, but the majority of them are mid-to-lower-level public relations practitioners. PRSA is headquartered in New York, and IABC is based in San Francisco.

As we have pointed out previously (Wright, 1995, 1998), other research studying occupational roles in public relations has identified the role of communication executives, most of whom have direct access to the C-suite and, in many cases, report to corporate CEOs. These public relations people operate at a much more senior level than that reported in the PRSA and IABC role studies.

Closely linked to the expansion of PR occupational roles to include the communication executive role is the fact that public relations practice today incorporates much more than media relations, an important part of public relations practice that somewhat dominated the field three or four decades ago.

Methodology

The study's methodology consisted of brief e-mail interviews with women holding truly senior-level PR/Comm. positions with Fortune 500 companies or major (top 25) public relations firms. All subjects were long-time members of the Arthur W. Page Society. The author of this chapter served more than 20 years on the Page Society Board of Trustees and was well known to the study's research subjects. Anonymity and confidentiality were promised to all research participants, and interviews were conducted with 18 subjects during February 2020. Not every subject answered every question. On average, participants in the study had spent 34 years working in various aspects of the public relations industry. Questions focused on gender equity, salaries, occupational role responsibilities, and perceived differences between the way women are treated as public relations executives vis-à-vis men.

Page considers itself the world's leading professional association for senior-level public relations and communications executives. The total membership numbers about 800 and consists of chief communications officers of global Fortune-ranked corporations, CEOs of the world's foremost public relations agencies, and distinguished academics from top business and communication schools. The society's mission is to strengthen the enterprise leadership role of the chief communications officer whilst its purpose is to unite the world's best communicators to transform business for the better.

Results

The results section reports on some, but not all, of the more meaningful comments collected during the interviews. The discussion section examines how the results of the current study differ from results of public relations gender research from a generation ago.

> **Responses to the question: How has your experience as a woman working in the communications and public relations industry changed from the start of your career until now?**
>
> *As I've grown in my career, I've found it easier to gain respect for what we do as professionals and how we do it. However, I have not seen as significant of an increase in the understanding of the position or its business value as I would have expected over a 30-year period. Because of this, it is still challenging for*

women to be seen as equal executives in companies where communications is considered a soft skill. Often, when female communication executives are fully respected as an equal executive partner, it is in spite of their communications leadership, not because of it.

At the start of my career, most of the leaders were men, but that has changed to include many more women in leadership roles or even the top communications role. I also believe more professional development and leadership growth opportunities exist now than when I began my career more than 30 years ago.

Today, women are in executive positions in most publicly-traded companies and many of the current top PR agency leaders are women.

Opportunities for women have grown dramatically since I entered the communications profession.

Responses to the question: Do you perceive any differences between how men and women are treated in the PR field?

I have not felt I was treated differently; if I was, it was to my benefit.
Absolutely! When a man is the senior PR professional, the communications profession often is taken more seriously.

Early on, my perception was that my male counterparts were brought into conversations earlier than my female counterparts, who tended to be brought in when there were actual tactics to be completed. Men were more relied on for a strategic view and women were more the "task takers" who created the communication and saw to the details of approvals and distributions.

Years ago I would have responded, "Yes" to this question but many things have changed and things are much better today than they used to be.

Responses to the question: Have you personally ever been treated differently in your career because you are a woman?

Are you kidding? It is the norm, not the exception.
If I was treated differently it was to my benefit.
Early on (in the 1980s), men didn't know how to treat women the same. For example, the men could chide other men but didn't dare do that to a woman. Men were careful in their language in front of women. That has changed in my view but you are better off asking men.

This only happened once but I was asked for input and, instead of asking me my thoughts on a strategic approach, the questioner prefaced the outreach with "we need a feminine viewpoint".

Yes. Twice in my career I received maternity leave benefits that were not available to my male colleagues.

Responses to the question: Some of the academic research on gender differences in the PR/Comm. industry suggests women have been paid substantially less than men, even when other variables are controlled. Have you found this to be true?

I have no evidence that this is true; I only have anecdotal gossip so I'm not able to say definitively.

I haven't a clue. I have been well compensated in my opinion, based on the information I have seen.

Earlier in my career the discrepancy was much greater than it is now. I credit a large part of this improvement being due to more women in leadership roles who are focused on improving gender pay equity.

Responses to the question: These same research studies indicate women who work in PR/Comm. are more likely to perceive themselves as filling a technical role than a managerial or executive one. Have you found this to be true?

No. However, in my career I have always set out to define what success looks like and it has never been a transactional or technical role.

Not at all. However, I do believe women (and men) in PR/Comm. do not approach the role or issues from a strategic perspective or with an understanding of the way the business works, are not included when executives discuss strategic issues. I also believe that is a failing in our profession and that communication/PR students should be taught and be expected to know how business operates and not just how to be a great communicator.

The salary inequity situation can be viewed as a two-way street. Regardless of gender, those willing to accept high-paying, executive-level communications positions must be willing to make certain sacrifices not everyone is willing to make. Those who want evenings and weekends off really shouldn't apply for such positions.

The way I would answer this question is to say that 10 years ago, if a woman was placed in this role, it was viewed as a head of function. Today we are seeing more women leading communication/PR who have broader roles in corporate strategy, corporate reputation, corporate culture and the Employee Experience and are being leaned on by the C-suite as more of a counsellor to the business than "just" head of function.

Not any more. Although this used to be the norm, things have changed in the PR/Comm. world and this sort of thing isn't a problem anymore.

Discussion

The women public relations executives interviewed in the study reported in this chapter have had more positive experiences working in the public relations industry than the subjects in the original "velvet ghetto" and "glass ceiling" studies three or four decades ago. As one subject explained, "Opportunities for women have grown dramatically since I entered the communications profession." Another told us, "Today, women are in executive positions in most publicly-traded companies and many of the current PR agency leaders are women."

It is probably important to note that the public relations function has changed dramatically during the past three or four decades, growing from a field that used to focus on media relations by helping clients and organizations answer the question, "How should we say it?" Today's industry focuses more on, "What should be done? How should we do it?", and "What should we say?" Even though the current study strongly suggests a clear trend indicating things are better in the public relations workplace than they used to be, results continue to reflect comments such as, "When a man is the senior PR professional, the communications profession often is taken more seriously."

Subjects in the current study were extremely firm in their answers when asked if they perceived themselves as communication technicians or communication managers. When asked if they felt they were technicians, the responses included "Not at all", "No," and "Not anymore."

Comments about salary differences were considerably more friendly and gentle than was the case with the earlier studies. As one subject explained, "Earlier in my career, the discrepancy was much greater than it is now. I credit a large part of this improvement being due to more women in leadership roles, who are focused on improving gender pay equity."

There is also a strong message in the comment, "The salary inequity situation can be viewed as a two-way street. Regardless of gender, those willing to accept high-paying, executive-level communications positions must be willing to make certain sacrifices not everyone is willing to make. Those who want evenings and weekends off really shouldn't apply for such positions."

Limitations

As mentioned previously, the results of this study are based on interviews with only 18 subjects. "Many things have changed and things are much better than they used to be."

Conclusion

This study of e-mail interviews with senior-level women working in the public relations and corporate communication industry found oppurtunities for women and the status of women in public relations has improved considerably from the era of the "Velvet Ghetto" and "Glass Ceiling" research reports from three or four decades ago. Although the situation today might not be perfect, many agree things are better than they used to be. In the words of one of this study's respondents, "We've come a long way but we've still got a long way to go."

References

Aldoory, L., Jiang, H., Toth, E.L. & Sha, B. (2008). Is it still just a women's issue? A study of work-life-balance among men and women in public relations. *Public Relations Journal*, 2(4).

Bates, D. (1983). A concern: Will women inherit the profession? *Public Relations Journal*, 39(7), 6–7.

Bernstein, J. (1987). Is PR field being hurt by too many women? *Advertising Age*, (January 27), 6.

Broom, G. M., & Dozier, D.M. (1986). Advancement for public relations role models. *Public Relations Review*, 12(1), 37–56.

Cline, C.G., Masel-Walters, L., Toth, E.L., Turk, J.V., Smith, H.T., & Johnson, N. (1986). *The velvet ghetto: The impact of the increasing percentage of women in public relations and organizational communication.* San Francisco: IABC Foundation.

Creedon, P.L. (1991). Public relations and women's work: Toward a feminist analysis of public relations roles, *Public Relations Research Annual*, 3, 67–84.

Dozier, D.M. (1988). Breaking public relations' glass ceiling, *Public Relations Review*, 14(3), 6–14.

Dozier, D.M., Sha, B., Shen, H. (2013). Why women earn less than men: The cost of gender discrimination in U.S. public relations. *Public Relations Journal*, (7)1.

Fidelzeid, G. (2015, March 2). How to close the gender pay gap in PR. *PR Week*. www.prweek.com/article/1335944/close-gender-pay-gap-pr. Accessed July 22, 2015.

Grunig, L.A. (1988). A research agenda for women in public relations, *Public Relations Review*, 14(3), 18–57.

Hon, L.C., Grunig, L.A., & Dozier, D.M. (1992). Women in public relations: Problems and opportunities, 419–438 in Grunig, J.E. (Ed.), *Excellence in public relations and communication management.* Hillsdale, NJ: Lawrence Erlbaum.

PRWeek. (2015). www.prweek.com/article/1264912/diversity-agency-leadership-remains-debate. Accessed January 21, 2020.

Sha, A. (2015). "Why aren't there more female CEOs in PR"? *Holmes Report*. (April). Accessed at: www.holmesreport.com/long-reads/article/why-aren't-there-more-female-ceos-in-pr.

Taff, H.P. (2003). Times have changed. IABC research foundation's "The Velvet Ghetto" study revisited. *Communication World*, 20(2), 10–11.

Theus, K.T. (1985). Gender shifts in journalism and public relations, *Public Relations Review*, 11(1), 42–50.

Toth, E.L. (1988). Making peace with gender issues in public relations. *Public Relations Review*, 14(3), 36–47.

Toth, EW.L. & Cline, C.G., Eds. (1989). *Beyond the velvet ghetto.* San Francisco: IABC Research Foundation.

Toth, E.L. & Grunig, L.A. (1993). The missing story of women in public relations, *Journal of Public Relations Research*, 5(3), 153–175.

Wright, D.K. (1995). The role of corporate public relations executives in the future of employee communications. *Public Relations Review*, 21(3), 181–198.

Wright, D.K (1998). Validating credibility measures of public relations and communications: Interviews with senior-level managers and executives from other corporate disciplines. *Journal of Communication Management*, 3(2). 105–118.

Wright, D.K., Grunig, L.A., Springston, J.K. & Toth, E.L. (1991). *Under the glass ceiling: An analysis of gender issues in American public relations.* New York: Public Relations Society of America Foundation Monograph Series, 1(2).

Wrigley, B.J. (2002). Glass ceiling? What glass ceiling? A qualitative study on how women view the glass ceiling in public relation and communications management, *Journal of Public Relations Research*, 14(1), 27–55.

Zoch, L.M. & Russell, M.P. (1991). Women in PR education: An academic "velvet ghetto"? *Journalism Educator*, 46(3), 25–35.

2 Women in public relations
A thematic analysis of ECM data (2009–2019)

Martina Topić and Ralph Tench

Introduction

According to all available research, women in the communications industry face disadvantages; for example, in advertising, public relations and journalism, women began outnumbering men in the industry decades ago. However, they are still facing the glass ceiling and the pay gap, as well as sexism and discrimination (CIPR, 2019; Place and Vaderman-Winter, 2018; Topić, 2018; Crewe and Wang, 2018; Yaxley, 2013; Sleeman, 2019; UK Digital and Creative Sector Talent Insight Report, 2017; Stein, 2017).

In the advertising industry, scholars have recognised issues, such as the industry being slow to change. Creative departments are still predominantly staffed by men, and there seems to be a recognition of the 'old-boys' mentality and (homo)-sociality (Grow and Yang, 2018; Weisberg and Robbs, 1997; Broyles and Grow, 2008; Crewe and Wang, 2018). In journalism, on the other hand, an issue of masculinity was recognised as a prevalent factor decades ago that has continued until the present day. For example, Graber (1980) argued that women have to merge into male-controlled newsrooms and the masculine newsroom culture. This means that while the number of women working in journalism has increased exponentially, the news values and information-gathering technique have never changed (Christmas, 1997). Some authors also argued that journalism's culture is so masculinised that women who stay in the journalistic profession and progress to senior roles 'become so "bloke-ified" by the macho water in which they swim that many younger women looking up don't see them as role models for the kind of women they might want to become' (Mills, 2014: 17). Nevertheless, some authors also found that even when the so-called feminine topics, to which women have been confined for decades, enter the public agenda and the main news section, it is men who start writing about them (Topić, 2018).

In this chapter, we are focusing on women in public relations and their distinctive position within the public relations industry. To that end, we are analysing available literature and then moving on to analyse data from the European Communications Monitor collected in the period from 2009 to 2019, thus providing a decade of trends among practitioners in European public relations practice relating to the position of women in the industry.

Women in public relations

Women in public relations is a theme of research that first appeared in 1968,[1] becoming more prominent among public relations scholars since 1982 when the first larger studies started to appear. Since 1982, more than 200 research studies have been produced. For example, Topić et al. (2019) analysed 223 articles published between 1982 and 2019 in English, Portuguese, Spanish, French, Croatian, Serbian, Slovenian, Dutch and Georgian. They identified trends and issues reported in the literature per decade of research (1980–1989, 1990–1999, 2000–2009 and 2010–2019). The analysed literature predominantly related to practitioners; that is, scholars were mostly reporting findings on surveys, interviews and focus groups they conducted with practitioners, thus providing an overview of issues in public relations industries.

As the analysis has shown, the unfavourable position of women in public relations has turned full circle, with the same issues that were being reported in the 1980s returning to the scene during the last analysed period, 2010–2019 (Topić et al., 2019). Therefore, during the 1980s scholars reported that women face work discrimination (glass ceiling, pay gap, technician positions for women and educational differences between men and women) and bias (covert discrimination in promotions, chauvinism, stereotypes against women and feminisation). In practice, this meant that women were facing a glass ceiling (Broom, 1982; VanSlyke, 1983; Scrimger, 1985; Cline et al, 1986; Pratt, 1986; Dozier, 1988) and a pay gap (VanSlyke, 1983; Cline et al, 1986; Miller, 1988; Lance Toth, 1988; Dozier, 1988; Singh and Smyth, 1988). This was, in large part, due to the fact women were confined to technician positions, whereas men were fulfilling more managerial roles, thus enabling them to progress in their careers (Broom, 1982; Cline et al., 1986).

Besides, women were reported to be more likely to join the industry with a degree in public relations, whereas men mostly joined with a degree in journalism (Theus, 1985). The bias was manifested in covert discrimination for promotions, such as creating new role titles to enable the promotion of men, which then also contributed towards the pay gap (Cline et al., 1986; Scrimger, 1985). In addition, women faced chauvinism, such as being seen as a flight risk, as it was believed that women would leave their job if their husband's career takes them elsewhere. Furthermore, stereotypes against women were openly promoted, such as 'not suitable to be good managers, too emotional, lacking corporate spirit, not being good team members and simply not part of the gang' (Topić et al., 2019: 17). This is why some authors called public relations a 'pink ghetto' because, while women were allowed into the industry, they had no real influence or power within public relations organisations (Cline et al., 1986).

Fast forward to the period between 2010 and 2019 and it transpires that the same discrimination returned to the public relations scene, as the analysis of literature conducted by Topić et al. (2019) showed. The main themes in academic research conducted on practitioners were the same, work discrimination and bias against the women, albeit with some tweaks. For example, work discrimination now also includes recognition of the lack of diversity and masculinity in an organisation (ibid), as scholars are increasingly recognising these issues. However, the issues of the glass ceiling and the pay gap have remained (Dubrowski et al., 2019; Place and Varderman-Winter, 2018; Alemán et al., 2018; Tench and Topić, 2017; Soria and Gomez, 2017; Fitch and Third, 2010; Moreno et al., 2018a; Moreno et al., 2017; Moreno et al., 2015; Varderman-Winter and Place, 2017; Andrade and Sobreira, 2013). When it comes to bias against women, the latest period includes stereotypes about women's organisational and communications skills (Topić et al., 2019).

In other words, women in the 1980s faced the prejudice of 'not being suitable to be good managers, too emotional, lacking corporate spirit, not being good team members and simply not part of the gang' (Topić et al., 2019: 17). However, the prejudice against women in the last decade shifted to the belief that men have better organisational skills, whereas women have stronger media and communication skills and relationship-building skills (Lee et al., 2018; Verhoeven and Aarts, 2020). Thus, while the nature of the prejudice has changed with time, prejudice against women remains, and they seem to be deprived of career progress and equality of opportunities. Some scholars also noted that a significant role in this process is also being played by popular culture, where women are often portrayed as a love interest, young, desirable and single, whereas men are portrayed as untrustworthy or unhelpful; thus, popular culture contributes towards the degradation of the public relations field as a whole (Fitch, 2015; Johnston, 2010).

Nevertheless, the European Communication Monitor (ECM) annually surveys practitioners and asks them, inter alia, about their gendered perceptions of work in the public relations and communications industry. Tench and Topić (2017) previously analysed the ECM surveys in the period from 2009 to 2015, and they found that, as one issue gets resolved, a new issue emerges. For example, women participating in the ECM first reported that men dominate higher positions, and women face a glass ceiling and lack influence in the department; as the ECM survey progressed, practitioners started to report better job security for men and a lack of mentorship opportunities for women to develop into leaders. In other words, as one issue started to improve (e.g. the glass ceiling), a new issue emerged (e.g. mentoring and job security) (Tench and Topić, 2017).

Method

In this paper, we are continuing the research we previously conducted (Tench and Topić, 2017) to consider data published after 2015 and to re-analyse ECM findings to provide a picture of the position of women in public relations in the ECM in a period from 2009 to 2019. Thus, a full decade of research on women's perceptions of their position in the public relations and communications industry will be captured.

The European Communications Monitor[2] is the largest and longest-running survey worldwide that monitors trends in the public relations and communications

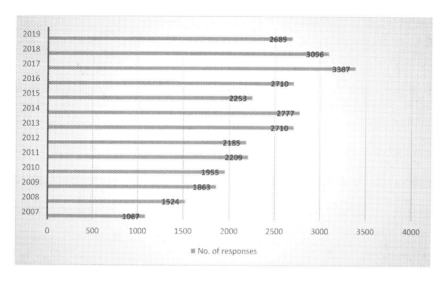

Figure 2.1 Responses in ECM surveys per year.

industries in Europe, having been conducted annually since 2007. Since 2009, the survey also monitors the position of women in the industry. Each year, thousands of practitioners participate in the survey (Figure 2.1), thus providing a good overview of the experiences, feelings and perceptions of practitioners working in the field.

In each annual survey, 'the PR practitioners are asked to report on issues in the field, predict future development of the field, as well as to report on difficulties and inequality between male and female practitioners should they believe that inequality exists' (Tench and Topić, 2017: 9). Gender issues have been included in all annual ECM surveys, except in 2013.

Participants are regularly recruited from up to 50 European countries each year via personal invitations sent to professionals using email and sourced from the member database provided by the European Association of Communication Directors, as well as personal networks of the research team and the national coordinators and national branches of public relations associations across Europe.

The ECM consortium publishes a detailed report/book and video in May or June each year with the findings from the annual survey; this book and other support materials are available from the project website: www.communicationmonitor.eu/european-communication-monitor-all-reports/.

For this chapter, we have downloaded these brochures and analysed data about the position of women in the industry to look at the results collectively and to discuss whether circumstances are changing for women in public relations and the communications industries.

The ECM is not longitudinal research because the number of participants varies (Figure 2.1) between years, and the responses are anonymous; therefore, we do not know who the participants are and whether, for example, the same participants took the survey in each survey year or are unique for each year. Therefore, this chapter does not claim to offer any generalisation of results. Instead, we are conducting a trends analysis research using thematic analysis method to capture trends and reported issues in the public relations and communications industries over ten years (2009–2019). Besides, questions are not the same in each ECM survey but depend on the trends identified by the research team in practitioner and academic literature, which then feeds into every annual survey. Additionally, some gender data emerges from other questions; for example, questions in 2018 included stress at work due to growing debates on workers' well-being and increased workloads around the world. This then resulted in a different response from men as opposed to women, which was then captured in the results.

In this chapter, we are analysing all data concerning gender that has emerged over the years. To that end, we accumulated data in groups, and, thus, we analysed the glass ceiling, salaries (pay gap) and general differences between men and women in perceiving and handling work issues.

The research questions set for the chapter were:

- Which data on gender was observed in the period between 2009 and 2019?
- Are there differences in the work experiences between men and women?
- Are the surveyed women reporting equality of opportunities?

We used thematic analysis to analyse and present the findings, following Braun and Clarke's (2006) approach to thematic analysis. This means that we analysed all ECM brochures with results of annual ECM surveys and then we divided the findings into the main themes. The thematic analysis can be defined as:

> a systematic approach to the analysis of qualitative data that involves identifying themes or patterns of cultural meaning; coding and classifying data, usually textual, according to themes; and interpreting the resulting thematic structures by seeking commonalities, relationships, overarching patterns, theoretical constructs or explanatory principles.
>
> (Lapadat 2010: 926)

The thematic analysis is a form of sense-making approach, and it is particularly helpful for researchers handling large data sets (Rohwer and Topić, 2018) or for comparing data as we did with the analysis of ECM data. The advantage of thematic analysis is that it also helps in depicting where further research is necessary and capturing trends, with which it becomes a useful tool for researchers who wish to explore the field further, find research gaps and add to the existing knowledge.

Women in PR: a thematic analysis of ECM

All of the published books from the annual ECM surveys have been researched, and all data about the position of women have been extracted and analysed for this chapter to identify the main themes and incorporate practitioners' views on the position of women in the public relations and communications industries in Europe.

Due to the low resolution of figures in ECM reports, it was not possible to copy figures from reports to visualise the analysis. To avoid text-heavy description of figures, the figures from ECM reports are quoted in the text, and page numbers from each report are used. The direct links to ECM reports are in the list of references.

Findings

The results appear to indicate that two predominant themes emerge from the ECM surveys, which are: (1) the glass ceiling and the pay gap and (2) the work environment (manifested through sub-themes of stress, lack of power in departments, heavy workloads, different online skills and understanding of social bots and different visual competencies).

Theme 1: The glass ceiling and the pay gap

In this theme, practitioners observed that men dominated higher positions in 2009, especially higher positions in public relations and communications organisations, whereas, in 2014, practitioners reported higher status within the organisation and job security for men. For example, in 2009, men were more present in the head of communication and CEO roles, whereas women were more present in roles such as unit leader and team member (ECM, 2009: 14).

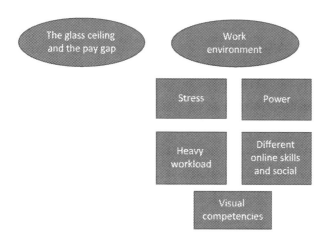

Figure 2.2 Thematic map of main themes in ECM surveys (2009–2019).

In 2014, women expressed dissatisfaction with work by showing less enthusiasm for work. In that, women showed more disagreement with statements on work balance, salary, job security, the appreciation of work by superiors and satisfaction with work (ECM, 2014: 40). This is a historical problem in the public relations industry, and scholars have observed this issue since intensifying scholarships about women in public relations (Cline at al., 1986; Topić et al., 2019).

With regards to gender differences, pay gap data is the most consistently recorded data in the ECM, appearing in every annual sample except in 2012, 2013 and 2019. In every observed sample, it is possible to find differences in income between men and women with men holding the monopoly on the higher earning positions. The situation changes slightly as time progresses; however, the difference remains. Nevertheless, in the year 2018, the ECM records a significant pay gap between men and women in higher positions, thus signalling that even when women do manage to break the glass ceiling, they are still undervalued and paid less (ECM, 2009: 84; ECM, 2010: 107; ECM, 2011: 130; ECM, 2014: 127; ECM, 2015: 101; ECM, 2016: 103; ECM, 2017: 103; ECM, 2018: 111).

Theme 2: Work environment

In this theme, several observations on differences in perceptions and observations of the work environment, as well as differences in skills, have been recorded amongst practitioners. Therefore, women working in public relations and communication reported a lack of influence in the department in 2012 (ECM, 2012, p. 60), which is in line with literature where scholars have been reporting this issue since 1982 (Topić et al., 2019; Cline et al., 1986; Broom, 1982; VanSlyke, 1983; Scrimger, 1985).

However, the main differences seem to arise from differences in job roles and competencies. For example, female practitioners reported in 2016 spending more time on operational communication, as opposed to men reporting they are involved in the alignment process, such as managing communication activities and co-workers (ECM, 2016: 48). This is in line with the literature since the 1980s that reports women can be found predominantly confined to technician roles (Cline et al., 1986; Topić et al., 2019).

This also leads to the difference in skills where online skills, for example, differ in various dimensions, and it is visible that women report higher skills in roles that can be seen as a technician, such as delivering messages via social media. This is opposed to men who report higher skills in roles that require managerial experience, such as knowing how to avoid risks and handling a crisis, which was reported in 2016 (ECM, 2016: 88). However, what is relevant to emphasise is that women do report fewer skills in more strategic roles, but this can be seen to result from a lack of mentorship and experience, which has already been reported in relevant research (Tench and Topić, 2017; Topić, 2019). This then also leads to the situation of men reporting higher competencies in visual skills, such as design, animation, professional photography and professional video editing, which was reported in 2017 (ECM, 2017: 38).

Men also tend to perceive social bots more than women do, particularly in regards to bots as a threat to the reputation of the organisation, which belongs to the domain of strategic communications and management traditionally occupied by men (ECM, 2017: 48).

Finally, two of the most recent ECM surveys report on the work conditions and views and experiences of men and women, in light of the growing interest of scholars and the public about work environments and the well-being of staff. Therefore, female practitioners reported in 2018 having more stress and fewer resources to manage it than men have (ECM, 2018: 77), whereas, in 2018, female practitioners labelled the stress at work as serious (ECM, 2018: 81). This data on its own would not call for much attention; however, the ECM from 2018 reports that the lack of resources is generally present at middle positions in the organisational hierarchy, which is where most of the women are centred (ECM, 2018). Thus, this is showing that the glass ceiling and unequal distribution of power and opportunities have an impact on general well-being.

Nevertheless, women particularly assess having a too-heavy workload and constant availability outside of working time via mobile phone and email as being stressful (ECM, 2018: 85), which corresponds with findings in some other studies. For example, Topić and Bruegmann (2020) interviewed 20 women working in journalism in the UK, and many reported especially the sense of constant working and workload as stressful. This is showing that the communication industry(ies) suffer(s) from a heavy workload and a lack of free time, which contributes towards general well-being and career prospects. It seems that this issue in public relations is particularly inherent to the experiences of women, at least when the ECM findings are taken into account. Not surprisingly, women practitioners expressed, in the same year, having less job satisfaction than men, which is in line with the general perception of stress due to heavy workloads and a lack of free time (ECM, 2018: 94).

Finally and perhaps most relevant to putting other data in a context is the data arising from the ECM for 2019 where women reported trust and a good relationship with external stakeholders, whereas men reported a good relationship with top leaders (ECM, 2019: 30). This immediately begs a question of whether heavy workloads and less job satisfaction have a lot to do with the fact men have connections at the top of organisations, which can reduce their workload, as well as indicate spare resources in their departments. Meanwhile, women are left to cope with what is left of resources and to struggle with work pressure. The fact that men have these contacts is a historical issue well known in organisational studies and not just in the communications industries but more generally. Men have historically formed the so-called 'boys clubs' and 'old-boy' mentality (Crewe and Wang, 2018), and this has had an impact on the experiences of women in the industry.

Conclusion

In this chapter, we have continued our previous research of ECM data (Topić and Tench, 2017) and analysed a decade of ECM survey data to capture the main data on the position of women in the public relations and communications industries. While our first research found that when one issue gets resolved, new issues emerged (ibid), this re-analysis has confirmed those findings and has intensified them by pointing that the discrimination continues, which is in line also with the major analysis of the literature review conducted by Topić et al. (2019). In other words, this new analysis of the ECM data has shown that within a decade, women continually report issues with inequality. While first women reported inequality being demonstrated consistently through the pay gap and glass ceiling, they also started to report issues within organisations, such as stress, a too-heavy workload and a lack of resources as time progressed. What remained constant throughout the survey period is the pay gap, which looked as if it improved in our first analysis; however, when a decade was analysed, a different situation emerged. This finding is in line with other literature where scholarly work has shown that the discrimination of women has travelled full circle, and women still face workplace discrimination, bias and prejudices (Topić et al., 2019).

Therefore, to answer the research questions posited at the start of this chapter, the data observed in the period from 2009 to 2019 were collated into two themes: (1) the pay gap and the glass ceiling and (2) the work environment, with the second issue also having sub-themes of stress, heavy workload, different online skills, and different visual skills and power. This means that the data found in this analysis is mostly in line with existing research on women in public relations, as discussed in the literature review. The only difference is that this data shows more data normally analysed within the liberal feminist approach, such as pay gap and the glass ceiling, which is likely because of the European focus of the research. Conversely, other research quoted in the literature review section and a large literature report by Topić et al. (2019) is conducted predominantly in an individual national context. However, this data still shows some new trends in the position of women in public relations, such as stress, heavy workload and a lack of resources, which requires further exploration. The women surveyed over the decade of data discussed in the ECM findings consistently report the lack of equal opportunities and differences between men and women. In addition to the reported stress, a lack of resources on the middle level and heavy workloads, there is also a difference in the skill set between men and women such as visual communications, social bots and online skills. The raises a question of why women lack these skills and whether this has something to do with the lack of power within an organisation, as women already reported. In other words, women report a lack of influence and power, and they also report being able to develop good relations with external stakeholders while men report a good relationship with senior managers at the top of their organisational structures, which could be a reason for the lack of skills, training opportunities and resources for women employees and middle managers. The literature generally recognises the problems with the 'old-boy' networks and (homo)sociality (Crewe and Wang, 2018), and it seems clear that this needs to be included in further research on women in public relations to establish the extent women are being excluded from these networks and how these networks work in the digital age.

Notes

1 The full reference for this paper is Smith, R. W. (1968), Women in public relations. *Public Relations Journal* 24(10), 26–29. However, we have not been able to find a copy of this report; hence, we are not citing it in the reference list as it has not been used to underpin our chapter.
2 The European Communication Monitor is the largest transnational study on strategic communication worldwide. It has been conducted annually for over 15 years with more than 40,000 communication professionals participating. The North American Communication Monitor (NACM) and the Latin American Communication Monitor (LCM) are part of the Global Communication Monitor series, the largest regular global study in the field of strategic communication and public relations. The series has analysed trends in the field for more than a decade and covers more than 80 countries across Europe, North America, Latin-America and the Asia-Pacific region.

References

Alemán, I. I., Lazo, C. M. and del Olmo, F. J. R., La influencia del género en el management de la comunicación corporativa: Estudio de caso en Aragón (España), *Prisma Social: revista de investigación social* 20, 2018: 273–286.

Andrade, C. and Sobreira, R., Igualdade de género na profissão de relações públicas: estudo exploratório com estudantes de comunicação organizacional (Gender equity in the PR profession: exploratory study with organizational communication students), *EXEDRA Journal* 7, 2013: 41–50.

Braun, V. and Clarke, V., Using thematic analysis in psychology, *Qualitative Research in Psychology* 3(2), 2006: 77–101.

Broom, G. M., A comparison of sex roles in public relations, *Public Relations Review* 8(3), 1982: 17–22.

Christmas, L., Women in Journalism: Chaps of both sexes? – Women decision-makers in newspapers: Do they make a difference?" *Report for Women in Journalism Organisation*, 1997. Retrieved from http://womeninjournalism.co.uk/wp-content/uploads/2012/10/Chaps-of-both-Sexes.pdf.

CIPR, *State of the Profession*, 2019. Retrieved from www.cipr.co.uk/sites/default/files/11812%20State%20of%20Profession_v12.pdf.

Cline, C., Toth, E., Turk, J., Walters, L, Johnson, N. and Smith, H., *The Velvet Ghetto: The Impact of the Increasing Percentage of Women in Public Relations and Business Communication*, IABC Foundation, 1986, USA.

Crewe, L. and Wang, A., Gender inequalities in the city of London advertising industry, *Environment and Planning A: Economy and Space* 50(3), 2018: 671–688.

Dozier, D. M, Breaking public relations glass ceiling, *Public Relations Review* 14(3), 1988: 6–14.

Dubrowski, M., McCorkindale and Rickert, R., *Mind the gap: Women's leadership in public relations*, 2019, Retrieved from https://instituteforpr.org/wp-content/uploads/IPR.KPMGWIL-Study-FINAL041219-compressed.pdf.

ECM (2009). *Results of the European Communication Monitor 2009.* Retrieved from www.communicationmonitor.eu/wp-content/uploads/2018/03/ECM-2009-Results-ChartVersion-European-Communication-Monitor-Trends-Strategic-Communication-Management-Corporate-Communication-Public-Relations-PR.pdf.

ECM (2010). *European Communication Monitor Results 2010.* Retrieved from www.communicationmonitor.eu/wp-content/uploads/2018/03/ECM-2010-Results-ChartVersion-European-Communication-Monitor-Trends-Strategic-Communication-Management-Corporate-Communication-Public-Relations-PR.pdf.

ECM (2011). *Results of the European Communication Monitor 2014.* Retrieved from www.communicationmonitor.eu/wp-content/uploads/2018/03/ECM-2011-Results-ChartVersion-European-Communication-Monitor-Trends-Strategic-Communication-Management-Corporate-Communication-Public-Relations-PR.pdf.

ECM (2012). Results of the European Communication Monitor 2012. Retrieved from www.communicationmonitor.eu/wp-content/uploads/2018/03/ECM-2012-Results-ChartVersion-European-Communication-Monitor-Trends-Strategic-Communication-Management-Corporate-Communication-Public-Relations-PR.pdf.

ECM (2014). *Results of the European Communication Monitor 2014.* Retrieved from www.communicationmonitor.eu/wp-content/uploads/2018/03/ECM-2014-Results-ChartVersion-European-Communication-Monitor-Trends-Strategic-Communication-Management-Corporate-Communication-Public-Relations-PR.pdf.

ECM (2015). Results of European Communication Monitor 2015. Retrieved from www.communicationmonitor.eu/wp-content/uploads/2018/03/ECM-2015-Results-ChartVersion-European-Communication-Monitor-Trends-Strategic-Communication-Management-Corporate-Communication-Public-Relations-PR.pdf.

ECM (2016). Results of European Communication Monitor 2016. Retrieved from www.communicationmonitor.eu/wp-content/uploads/2018/03/ECM-2016-Results-ChartVersion-European-Communication-Monitor-Trends-Strategic-Communication-Management-Corporate-Communication-Public-Relations-PR.pdf.

ECM (2017). Results of European Communication Monitor 2017. Retrieved from www.communicationmonitor.eu/2017/06/04/ecm-european-communication-monitor-2017-social-bots-visualisation-hypermodernity-benchmarking-strategic-communication/.

ECM, Key Insights (2018). European Communication Monitor 2018. Retrieved from www.communicationmonitor.eu/2018/06/13/ecm-european-communication-monitor-2018/.

ECM (2019). *Results of the European Communication Monitor 2019.* Retrieved from www.communicationmonitor.eu/wp-content/uploads/dlm_uploads/ECM19-European-Communication-Monitor-2019.pdf.

Fitch, K., Promoting the Vampire Rights Amendment: Public relations, post-feminism and true blood, *Public Relations Review* 41(5), 2018: 607–614.

Fitch, K. and Third, A., Ex-Journos and promo girls: Feminization and professionalization in the Australian public relations industry. In Daymon, C. & Demetrious, K. (eds.) *Gender and Public Relations: Critical Perspectives on Voice, Image and Identity.* Routledge, London, 2014, pp. 247–268.

Graber, D., *Crime News and the Public*, Praeger, 1980, New York.

Johnston, J., Girls on screen: How film and television depict women in public relations, *PRism* 7(4), 2010, Retrieved from www.prismjournal.org/fileadmin/Praxis/Files/Gender/Johnston.pdf.

Lance Toth, E., Making peace with gender issues in public relations, *Public Relations Review* 14(3), 1988: 36–47.

Lapadat, J., Thematic analysis. In *Encyclopaedia of case study research*, Mills, A. J., Durepos, G., & Wiebe, E. (eds), 2010, (pp. 926–928). Thousand Oaks: Sage.

Lee, H., Place, K. R. and Smith, B. G., Revisiting gendered assumptions of practitioner power: An exploratory study examining the role of social media expertise, *Public Relations Review* 44(2), 2018: 191–200.

Miller, D. A., Women in public relations graduate study, *Public Relations Review* 14(3), 1988: 29–35.

Mills, E., Why do the best jobs go to men? *British Journalism Review* 25(3), 2014: 17–23.

Moreno, A., Fuentes, C. and Khalil, N., *Gendercoms. Brechas y oportunidades de género en la profesión de Gestión de la Comunicación en España*, Asociación de Directivos de Comunicación, 2018a, Madrid.

Moreno, A., Molleda, J. C., Athaydes, A., Suárez, A. M., Herrera, M. and Álvarez Nobell, A., *Latin American Communication Monitor 2016–2017, Tendencias en comunicación estratégica: big data, automatización, engagement, influencers, couching y competencias. Resultados de una encuesta en 17 países*. DIRCOM/EUPRERA, 2017, Madrid.

Moreno, A., Molleda, J.C., Athaydes, A. and Suárez, A.M., *Latin American Communication Monitor 2014- 2015. Excelencia en comunicación estratégica, trabajo en la era digital, social media y profesionalismo. Resultados de una encuesta en 18 países*, EUPRERA, 2015, Brussels.

Place, K. R. and Vardeman-Winter, J., Where are the women? An examination of research on women and leadership in public relations, *Public Relations Review* 44(1), 2018: 165–173.

Pratt, C., Professionalism in Nigerian public relations, *Public Relations Review* 12(4), 1986: 27–40.

Rohwer, L. and Topić, M., The communication of corporate–NGO partnerships: analysis of Sainsbury's collaboration with comic relief, *Journal of Brand Management* 26(1), 2018: 35–48.

Scrimger, J., Profile: Women in Canadian public relations, *Public Relations Review* 11(3), 1985: 40–46.

Singh, R. and Smyth, R., Australian public relations: status at the turn of the 21st century, *Public Relations Review* 26(4), 1988: 387–401.

Sleeman, C., The creative industries' gender equality secret has been exposed by big data, *World Economic Forum*, 2019. Retrieved from www.weforum.org/agenda/2019/08/gender-equality-secret-exposed-by-big-data/.

Soria, M. and Gómez, B., Análisis del rol profesional de mujeres y hombres en las agencias de publicidad españolas. Percepciones e integración de igualdad de oportunidades (Analysis of professional role of women and men in Spanish advertising agencies: perception and integration of equal opportunities), *Sphera Publica* 2(17), 2017: 167–193.

Stein, L., Advertising is Still a Boy's Club, *AdAge*, 31 May 2017. Retrieved from https://adage.com/article/news/advertising-a-boy-s-club/309166.

Tench, R. and Topić, M ., One step forward, two steps back? An analysis of public relations practitioners' views on the position of women in the PR industry (2009–2015), *Current Politics and Economics of Europe* 28(1), 2017: 83–105.

Theus, K. T., Gender shifts in journalism and public relations, *Public Relations Review* 11(1), 1985: 42–50.

Topić, M., Not Bloke-ified enough? Women journalists, supermarket industry and the debate on sugar in the British Press (2010–2015), *Newspaper Research Journal* 39(4), 2018: 433–442.

Topić, M. and Bruegmann, C., Women journalists in the UK Press: The key findings from a qualitative study, the research report, Leeds Beckett University, 2020. Retrieved from http://eprints.leedsbeckett.ac.uk/6436/1/WomenJournalistsInTheUKPressPV-TOPIC.pdf.

Topić, M., Cunha, M.J. Reigstad, A., Jelen-Sanchez, A., Diers Lawson, A., Polić, M., Moreno, A., Zurbano Berenguer, B., Damian-Gaillard, B., Sanz, P., Fuentes Lara, C., Cesarec Salopek, N., Saitta, E., Cruz, C., Simeunović Bajić, N., Vandenberghe, H., Bibilashvili, L. and Kaladze, N. (2019), Women in public relations – A literature review (1982–2019), *EUPRERA Report* Vol 1., No. 1, 2019, Creative Media and Communications Research Ltd. & EUPRERA. ISSN 2633–2353, Leeds/Brussels.

UK Digital and Creative Sector Talent Insight Report, 2017. Retrieved from https://dma.org.uk/uploads/ckeditor/UK_Digital_and_Creative_Sector_Report.pdf.

VanSlyke, J. K., On the job: Corporate communicators in the United States and the United Kingdom, *Public Relations Review* 9(3), 1983: 55.

Vardeman-Winter, J. and Place, K. R., Still a lily-white field of women: The state of workforce diversity in public relations practice and research, *Public Relations Review* 43(2), 2017: 326–336.

Verhoeven, P. and Aarts, N., How European public relations men and women perceive the impact of their professional activities, *PRism* 7(4), 2010. Retrieved from: www.prismjournal.org/fileadmin/Praxis/Files/Gender/Verhoeven_Aarts.pdf.

Yaxley, H., Career experiences of women in British public relations (1970–1989), *Public Relations Review* 39(2), 2013: 156–165.

3 'Signum authenticum' of women

Herstories in Turkey's public relations during the early years

Melike Aktaş, G. Senem Gençtürk Hızal and B. Pınar Özdemir

Introduction

In Turkey, the period between 1960 and 1980 is considered the 'institutionalization years' of public relations (Gençtürk Hızal, Özdemir and Aktaş, 2014). During this historical period, the first public relations education programmes were established within universities with public relations defined as a 'corporate practice' both in the private and public sectors. During the establishment of the field, women were among the pioneers contributing to the recognition, institutionalization, professionalization and internationalization of public relations, and they shaped understanding of the field through their activities in Turkey. The pioneering women were the first ones who were teaching and academically productive, taking positions in public relations departments of public institutions and carrying out public relations activities in the private sector.

Pioneer women entering public relations field in Turkey starting from late 1960s coincides with the feminization of public relations in the West. It should be mentioned that 1970s were also a period in which the number of women from higher status groups in respected professional occupations has increased in Turkey. Public relations was established as a reputable field of study and practice during the institutionalization years, so that attracted women having excellent qualifications. Starting from an early period, important roles and responsibilities were realized by women, and they have inspired and encouraged increasing number of female practitioners entering public relations.

This study introduces the professional women who were influential during the institutionalization period of public relations in Turkey and who have contributed to the professionalization process of the field, as well as highlighting their experiences during this process. With this purpose, semi-structured interviews were held with pioneering women in the field during 2012 and 2013 in Ankara and İstanbul using the following research questions:

1. How did women encounter the field of public relations during the late 1960s and 1970s?

2. What factors affected opportunities for women's engagement with public relations practices?
3. Are there any commonalities between these women that enabled them to enter the field?

Women in the institutionalization years of public relations

In Turkey, public relations has evolved from contemporary approaches to public administration. One of the most prominent names is Nermin Abadan (Unat). Abadan contributed to the introduction of public relations in academia with her translations and original work. She was born in 1921 in Vienna and studied law, working first at a newspaper after her graduation before starting her academic career in 1953 as an assistant at Ankara University, Faculty of Political Sciences. The concept of public relations came to the fore for the first time in Turkish academic literature as a section in the translation of Marshall Dimock's book *Amme İdaresinin Prensipleri* (Principles of Public Administration) undertaken by Abadan in 1954. The first public relations articles written in Turkish were Abadan's papers titled *Amme İdaresi ve Halkla Münasebet Mefhumu* (Public Administration and the Concept of Public Relations) in 1955 and *Modern Toplumlarda Halkla Münasebetler* (Public Relations in Modern Societies) in 1964. By her work, Abadan defined the Turkish equivalent of public relations; she ensured that the concept was understood, and the field was recognized academically and discussed. In addition, she served on the commission formed for the establishment of the first university programme providing public relations education in Turkey (SBF BYYO, no date: 5). Another pioneering woman who contributed to the development of public relations in the academic field is Birkan Uysal, who is the author of the first doctoral thesis in which the concept of public relations was used. Uysal completed her doctoral studies in 1974 in Ankara University, Faculty of Political Science with her thesis titled *Kamu Yönetiminde Halkla İlişkiler* (Public Relations in Public Administration); her academic texts focused on public relations in the context of political sciences.

Traces of women in practising public relations were not visible until the 1970s. When public relations was institutionalized in Turkey for the first time within public administration, many women participated in those public relations departments. However, rather than a strategic choice, women's employment in public sector public relations departments was aimed at undertaking routine work. Hence, it is difficult to see women's signatures during the first periods of public sector public relations practices. Birten Gökyay constitutes an exception, as she established the National Productivity Centre (NPC) Public Relations Unit. The events organized by this Centre brought public relations academics and public- and private-sector representatives together and were effective in the adoption of public relations. Gökyay also took the Chair of the Ankara Public Relations Association in 1996 and published the Association's *Public Relations Journal*.

The 1970s saw Turkey's initial engagement with global capitalism and the number of multinational corporations increased, as well as holding companies starting to blossom; consequently, public relations became the agenda due to the needs of the private sector. Following the multinational companies, holding companies started to establish public relations departments. However, the number of people with the public relations expertise and experience to meet the increasing demand of the private sector at this time was very low; therefore, pioneering women entered the field with their qualifications and made significant contributions to the development of public relations.

In 1972, the Public Relations Association of Turkey was established in İstanbul by 13 founding members, two of whom were women. Canan (Usman) Reeves and Ayşegül Dora have made important contributions to the professionalization of public relations in Turkey. Their motivation behind establishment of the Association was the need to formalize public relations practitioners' personal acquaintances on a professional platform; however, it was an important step for professionalization of the field in Turkey. First experiences of the professional body are mentioned as follows:

> All the occupations had associations. We wanted to know one another, know what we were doing, if there were areas we needed to improve ourselves, we wanted to do that ... Everyone would come together at the meetings, we would talk about what we did.
> (Interview with Canan Reeves, September 15, 2012)

> We used to say, let's set up this business, put it in order so it becomes a profession. This was what we always talked about in the process of establishing the Association.
> (Interview with Ayşegül Dora, June 29, 2012)

Betûl Mardin, who joined the Board of Directors of the Association in 1975 and took the chair in 1978, has been effective in public relations' recognition in Turkey, helping the field to earn its current reputation.

Betûl Mardin is an important figure for international public relations history and the community because of her outstanding contributions to the profession globally. Mardin became a member of the International Public Relations Association (IPRA) and was elected as president of the Public Relations Association of Turkey in 1978. Soon after her presidency in Turkey, Mardin tried to develop more intense relationships with international organizations. She explains her efforts during these years as follows:

> I became an IPRA member in 1978, I attended many conferences ... . In that period, Prof. Sam Black, who was one of the milestones of the public relations profession, was the Secretary General of IPRA. I talked to him and we organized conferences together, first in Istanbul and then in Izmir.

Mardin won an award from IPRA in 1979, and her success was reported as 'A Turkish Women Receives a Degree in Public Relations World Congress' headline in Turkish Newspapers (Anonymous, 1979: 5). Mardin's efforts to internationalize public relations efforts in Turkey gave rise to the organization of an IPRA event in İstanbul, and an international seminar about 'the role of public relations between countries having issues' brought several countries together in 1979. Betûl Mardin holds membership emeritus status from IPRA, which is granted to members 'who have played a distinguished part in the affairs of IPRA and made a substantial contribution to the advancement of the public relations profession' (IPRA, 2020).

It can be asserted that bravery, determination, strength, sociability and a challenging nature are the common characteristics of these women, which may also have enabled them to enter this new field at that time. The pioneering women's personal histories were full of exciting adventures; for instance, Ayşegül Dora states her experiences as follows:

> Because I was a journalist who travelled abroad a lot. Then the Shahs, Buttos ... I have incredible adventures. I went to Qatar from Kuwait on a camel in four or five days ... I stayed in Russia for 3 months; it was so adventurous. I taught at the University of Tehran in Iran for a year.

Betûl Mardin expresses that before she participated in public relations, her sociability encouraged her to undertake many works related to the field:

> When I started my working life, I did journalism, I created radio programs, I finished the TV course at the BBC and thus I made a name in broadcast programming. When I came to Ankara I taught at TRT, as well as establishing the TV-drama department ... After that, I resigned and came to Istanbul from Ankara. When I came, I looked for a job but I was actually an expert in broadcast programming.

Pioneering women in public relations in Turkey pursued their careers in public relations with a determination that made the name of the woman visible in public relations, academia, public administration and the private sector. For instance, Canan Reeves started in a public relations department, carried on studies on public relations in BP and subsequently retired from there. Ayşegül Dora went back to journalism after she left from the first public relations agency *A&B Tanıtım*; she later founded *Pen Ajans*, an advertising and public relations agency, before selling it to the international network agency Darcy. After she left *A&B Tanıtım*, Betûl Mardin founded *İmaj Halkla İlişkiler* in 1987, which continued its activities until 2018. Birten Gökyay continued her public relations career, which started at the NPC, in various institutions in public administration and concluded it in 1996 as the Public Relations and Project Coordinator of the Turkish Cooperation and Development Agency established within the Ministry of Foreign Affairs.

Meeting the field: routes to occupation

From male mentors to women and from women to women

Pioneering women's entry into the profession has been shaped by coincidences. The first women public relations practitioners participated in the field through male executives whom they regarded as mentors. When there was a lack of comprehensive understanding of the field, some of the top-level visionary and well-educated male executives realized the importance of the field and introduced the pioneering women into the profession having recognized their qualities. During its early years, public relations was understood as a way of managing media relations and a kind of protocol management; therefore, it was seen as a suitable occupation for women who had appropriate knowledge, skills and aptitudes. During that period, apprehension of public relations was limited, as it was interpreted on the bases of courtesy, codes of conduct and corporate representation; this conceptualization was making the public relations field suitable for women. Nevertheless, knowledge of a foreign language in that era, as well as writing and rhetoric skills, were considered basic technical competences of public relations, and, while guiding women to the profession, mentors did not overlook these qualifications. Male executives led young and educated women from the same social networks and whom they believed had the previously mentioned technical skills. For instance, Betûl Mardin mentions her acquaintance with public relations as follows:

> After I quit *TRT* in 1968, I have accidentally begun this profession. Those years, there was nobody but me. They did not know about public relations, if you ask me they did not know advertising either ... I came to Istanbul from Ankara. I looked for a job; in fact I was a broadcasting specialist. Then I went to *Akbank*, I wanted to do advertising. I knew the CEO before. I told him about my opinion but he had a different offer not knowing its title but his offer was public relations. He asked me to manage his relations with his employees; he said 'this is a new occupation'. Finally he called someone and they told me that the French name of this job is *relations publiques*. I wrote down the name on a piece of paper and went to the American Library and made researches and studied about it. Books that I used are now torn apart but I still keep them. Fortunately, when people heard that I was looking for a job, they started to call me and make offers. They asked me if I do this or that and occasionally eighty percent of them were public relations. They did not know about it, but I was getting to learn about it. ... As I said, they did not know that this was called public relations.

Ayşegül Dora's introduction to the field was through Rıdvan Menteş, a leading name of the period who was performing public relations for the Simavi family, owners of one of the most popular newspaper of the era, Hürriyet:

> After I returned from abroad, Mr. Rıdvan learned from his mother that I studied telecommunication ... Hürriyet took the job for the World Trade

Congress. I was at Hürriyet back then. Mr. Rıdvan called me and directed me on the public relations of this job.

Even though the pioneering women's entry into the field was influenced by male mentors, they became mentors and role models themselves in the following periods, paving the way for many women. For instance, the IPRA Chair, brought to Turkey in 1995 by Betûl Mardin, was taken by the new generation of women public relations practitioners, by Ceyda Aydede in 2003 and Zehra Güngör in 2014.

Betûl Mardin states that women's career in public relations was not an easy pathway:

> Taking women in public relations seriously took some time. In our firm, we are quite careful on this issues as a part of our firm's policies. When I discovered this profession, I underlined that 'I dedicate it to women' because women's occupational options were limited.

Educational backgrounds and contributions to the education

Pioneering women in public relations received undergraduate and post-graduate degrees in the field, such as political science, communication and economics from the United States and Europe, when studying abroad was considered a privilege in Turkey. During the early years, it was an important opportunity to travel abroad and get to know the field, learn its practices and to receive formal training for the occupation. It should be noted that some of the pioneering women had the opportunity to obtain a degree in public relations from abroad before academic education became established in Turkey. Ayşegül Dora attended the London School of Economics to study communication, which covered advertising, public relations and journalism. After completing her undergraduate degree in law in Istanbul University, Nermin Abadan Unat attended the University of Minnesota for her post-graduate studies. Betûl Mardin attended the BBC's course in the United Kingdom.

It can be said that a number of coincidences were instrumental in pioneering women's entry into the profession; however, after joining the field, they grasped the importance of public relations and made an effort to gain new skills and knowledge on this subject. They made personal efforts to improve themselves in public relations and mentioned that they eagerly read and researched publications about public relations, which they often brought from abroad. Some of these efforts were also supported institutionally. For instance, Birten Gökyay mentioned that she has visited several European countries as a part of her position in the public sector, and she had an opportunity to access important sources.

Starting from the early years of the profession, pioneer women recognized the importance of formal education in the field. For instance, Canan Reeves expresses her views in 1987 regarding education in a symposium, as follows:

> Is education necessary or not for those working in this field? According to one view it is not necessary, there are those who say, we are doing it, it works.

When there were no schools for this subject in Turkey, large organizations, especially international organizations, used to send their public relations staff to seminars and meetings in other countries. There is no such problem today. Therefore, a question like the one above is irrelevant. What needs to be done is the improvement of Schools of Press and Publication. For example, if there is any lack in foreign languages, applied studies etc., we should work to improve these together. In this meeting and the ones before this one; not just those who were not educated in public relations but also the ones who have refreshed their knowledge and had the chance to follow the latest developments in both this discipline and technology. Therefore, I suggest that these seminars continue and be open to all public relations staff.

(Usman Reeves, 1987: 234)

The pioneering women's sense of responsibility about public relations education created an environment that gave them a chance to train future professionals in public relations. For instance, Ayşegül Dora and Betûl Mardin have been teaching public relations courses at universities since the 1990s.

Foreign language skills

Another common characteristic of pioneering women in the field is their mastery of foreign languages. The requirement for a foreign language was frequently emphasized in the narratives of women in the field of public relations at that time. Women, who are pioneers of public relations, expressed that an important requirement for working in the multinational companies where the first public relations practices took place in the private sector was competence in using foreign languages. In addition, Turkish literature on public relations was newly formed in the 1960s, and knowledge of a foreign language was therefore necessary to reach and use resources on the subject.

Ayşegül Dora explains that, back then, it was a privilege to speak a foreign language:

To know a foreign language … To speak a foreign language was not a common thing that everyone could have. Foreign companies were seeking foreign language speaking people. But how many people could speak a foreign language at that time? Me, for example, there were only two women who could speak a foreign language in Babıâli …

Canan Reeves, who was working for British Petroleum, states that knowledge of a foreign language was almost a requirement for working as a public relations employee at a multinational company operating in Turkey at that time:

How can you work at a foreign place, at public relations for an English company? As public relations, you work directly with the general manager and they are English … Most of the time you are responsible for the guests coming from abroad. That is to say, if they need to be taken somewhere or if a contact is needed for them. It was impossible without knowing the language. I have never seen or met someone working in our sector, in public relations, without speaking a foreign language.

These views of pioneering women in the private sector are also accepted by the pioneers in academia. For instance, Birkan Uysal stated:

Being competent in a foreign language was very important. Private high school graduates, such as those who graduated from schools like *Galatasaray*, were very easily following foreign resources so their way was open ... their foreign language skills made it very easy for them to find jobs in the private sector.

The dominant foreign language at that time was English because it was the language used by multinational companies operating in Turkey at the period. Today, English and vocational English are compulsory courses in the public relations curriculum for undergraduate degrees in Turkey, and different options for foreign languages are given to accompany these. Competence in foreign languages is still accepted as one of the prerequisites for success in the field today.

Networks and experiences

Besides their educational backgrounds, pioneering women's high cultural and social capitals, personal skills, aptitudes acquired from their families, lifestyles and their social circles helped them to get into public relations and progress in this field. Canan Reeves expresses her family's contribution to her occupational practice as follows:

From poets and sociologists to doctors, foreign archaeologists and professors; whoever you can think of, used to come to our house ... The contacts I got through my family helped my profession. For example we knew a lot of people, you could ask for their help or take their opinion or, through them, we were able to invite a lot of people.

Due to the lack of experienced public relations professionals during the early years, having a background in communication-related works helped to build a career; most pioneering women had that experience, especially in journalism. For instance, before going to the United States for her graduate degree, Nermin Abadan worked at *Ulus* Newspaper, Ayşegül Dora was a reporter for *Cumhuriyet* Newspaper and Canan Reeves prepared a programme for the BBC's Turkish service. Ayşegül Dora explained how her journalism experience may have helped her personal development:

Journalism is such a thing that ... So the article is written, it appears in the newspaper the next day, you are not there the next day; I mean it is something consumed daily. Hence, in those years, of course there was no television yet. There was incredible competition. Due to the competition, it required extreme creativity. That is to say, you had to do something at any moment. On top of that, you are a woman. At that time at Babıâli there were 5 or 8 women. That's all, of course. Thus, you are in a great competition. Maybe because of that competition, it enlightened me.

During the institutionalization years of public relations in Turkey, understanding of public relations was predominantly based on press relations. Undoubtedly, having backgrounds in journalism facilitated them succeeding in public relations. The fact that pioneering women switched to public relations from journalism has posed an inspiring career plan for other women entering the profession in the coming years.

Conclusion

Perceptions, understandings and endeavours of pioneer women in Turkey have made significant contributions to public relations both as an academic field of study and a professional practice. Emergent demand and quest for public relations during late 1960s helped these pioneer women entering the field. It should be noted that, besides having excellent skills and qualifications, their high class status was the common characteristic which led them into the profession. Public relations was regarded as reputable field and practice during the institutionalization years which enabled pioneer women to access and progress in the profession. It seems that during the early years, class was an important facilitator and asset for women's entry to public relations.

There is a lack of substantial data about the evolution of women's status in the public relations during its progress in Turkey. Nevertheless, it is possible to argue that women professionals are still holding important positions in the field. The Public Relations Association of Turkey celebrated its 48th anniversary in 2020; it has seen eight presidential terms, five of which were served by women. The Association started its journey with two women, and today 70% of its members are women (TÜHİD, 2020). Meral Saçkan was a woman president of the Public Relations Association of Turkey between 2000 and 2002, and she started the Altın Pusula (Golden Compass) awards in order to support the development of the industry. Among 27 members of Communication Consultancies Association of Turkey, there are 19 women leaders (IDA, 2020). Besides, the future of the profession in Turkey will be predominantly women considering the high number of female students studying public relations and young female practitioners.

References

Abadan, N. (1955). Amme idaresi ve halkla münasebetler mefhumu Public administration and concept of public relations. *SBF Dergisi*, X (2), 171–185.

Abadan, N (1964). *Modern toplumlarda halkla münasebetler*. Public Relations in Modern Societies. Ankara: TODAİE.

Anonymous (1979) Halkla ilişkiler dünya kongresinde bir Türk kadını derece aldı (A Turkish women got a reward in public relations world congress) (1979, May 13). *Cumhuriyet*, 5.

Dimock, M. E. (1954). *Amme idaresinin prensipleri*. Principles of public administration (N. Abadan, Trans.). Ankara: Ankara Üniversitesi Siyasal Bilgiler FakÜltesi Yayınları.

Gençtürk Hızal, G. S., Özdemir, B. P. & Aktaş Yamanoşlu, M. (2014). Tracking public relations history in 1960s' Turkey: The prevalence and reflections of development discourse. *Public Relations Review*, *40*(4), 632–638.

IDA (2020, May 5). Communication Consultancies Association of Turkey. Retrieved from www.ida.org.tr/ornek-sayfa/uyelerimiz/.

IPRA (2020, March 3). *The presidents of IPRA*. Retrieved from www.ipra.org/history/people/.

SBF BYYO (undated). *Kuruluş kitapçışı*. Foundation booklet. Ankara University Communication Faculty Archival material.

TÜHİD (2020, May 3). *Tühid Üyeleri*. Retrieved from www.tuhid.org/tuhid-uyeleri.html.

Usman Reeves, C. (1987). Türkiye'de halkla ilişkilerin gelişmesi için yapılabilecekler (Things to do for the development of public relations in Turkey). *Public Relations Symposium 87 Proceeding Book* (pp. 235–237). Ankara: Ankara Üniversitesi Siyasal Bilgiler Fakültesi Basın Yayın Yüksekokulu Basımevi.

4 Professional standards of PR in three decades through the lenses of Turkish women presidents of IPRA

Pelin Hürmeriç and A. Banu Bıçakçı

Introduction

Public relations (PR), a profession in constant change, has evolved from publicity-oriented practices into varying degrees of professionalization and sophistication with the democratization of the world in the latter half of the twentieth century (Sriramesh, 2003, p. xxix).

Professional associations, such as Public Relations Society of America (PRSA), International Public Relations Association (IPRA), International Association of Business Communicators (IABC) and European Confederation of Public Relations (CERP), paved the way to standardization of public relations and communication management practices. The role of women in this process is undeniable as there have been influential figures in the public relations industry throughout history. This chapter considers recent PR history through the prism of professionalization, based on the memoirs of three Turkish women presidents of IPRA.

In public relations literature, a number of research aim to analyse the roles and impact of women in the public relations profession (Broom, 1982; Toth & Grunig, 1993; Krider & Ross, 1997; Wrigley, 2002; Siler, 2009; Aldoory, 2009; Daymon & Demetrious, 2010; Creedon, 2011; Tsetsura, 2011a; Place, 2012; Grunig, Hon & Toth, 2013; Yaxley, 2013; Bıçakçı & Hürmeriç, 2013; Öksüz & Görpe, 2014; Fitch, James & Motion, 2016; Tench & Topić, 2017; Lee, Place & Smith, 2018). However, those studies often focus on gender roles and the challenges women PR practitioners face worldwide. Regarding the associations' points of view, two studies are related to women in the IABC (1986 and updated in 2003), but only one study (Mc Donald, 2009) focuses on women in a PR association (PRSA).

One of the most reputable associations relating to the public relations profession is IPRA, which was founded in London in 1955 (https://microsites.bournemouth.ac.uk/historyofpr/files/2011/11/IPRA-ARCHIVE-May-2015.pdf), with the aim of raising the standards of PR practice worldwide. The association has had a number of woman presidents in its 60-year history. In 1995, Betûl Mardin, already the first woman public relations practitioner in Turkey, became the first Turkish and Muslim president of IPRA, raising Turkey's profile within the public relations profession and increasing international co-operation in various PR projects (Bıçakçı & Hürmeriç, 2014, p. 263). By gaining international power, the PR profession in Turkey expanded from being local to being global; hence, this phase was nominated as the 'International competition phase' in Turkish PR history (Bıçakçı & Hürmeriç, 2013, p. 97). Then, Ceyda Aydede, who was president of a PR agency named the 'Global PR Agency', became the second Turkish IPRA President in 2003. The founder and president of the 'Stage PR Agency', Zehra Güngör, became the third Turkish and 50th IPRA President in 2014 (Bıçakçı & Hürmeriç, 2013, p. 98). The period since 2002 is marked as the most recent historical development phase and known as the 'Integration Phase'. Technological developments facilitated integration of the Turkish PR sector with other parts of the world, mainly the United States and Europe; however, scientific research and strategic thinking are still undervalued (Bıçakçı & Hürmeriç, 2013). While Betûl Mardin was active in the International Competition phase, Ceyda Aydede and Zehra Güngör are also representatives of the Integration Phase.

As Sriramesh and Duhé (2009, p. 368) asserted, the public relations activities of organizations are affected from the combination of social, political and economic forces that are powerful and pervasive. Hence, taking the political-economy approach of public relations into consideration, this chapter scrutinizes the progressive elaboration of public relations practice from the perspectives of three Turkish women IPRA presidents' within the three decades (1990s, 2000s and 2010s). The methodology is based on narrative analysis of semi-structured interviews held by telephone and e-mail, and the questions are derived and adapted from Li et al.'s (2012) study. The mentioned dates, names and facts expressed by the interviewees are checked through official websites, annual company reports, academic resources, media archives, curricula and other published interviews conducted with PR professionals in order to minimize the subjectivity of the collected data.

Professional standards within the evolution of PR

Public relations, as a twentieth-century phenomenon, is strongly influenced by social, cultural, economic and political advancements. Hence, it can be said that globalization, democratization and economic liberalization have important roles in the evolution of public relations (Sriramesh, 2003). Coombs and Holladay (2014, p. 123) claim that globalization, spurred by technological and economic developments, has provided both the opportunity and necessity of considering the role of public relations in creating a better society.

Mellado and Barría (2012) claim that as a profession, public relations and professional roles in public relations have been analysed by the literature as the normative and real functions of public relations practice that guides individuals' behaviour within an organizational context. In 1994, Wylie argued (as cited in Cameron et al., 1996, p. 44) interdisciplinary guidelines for a 'profession' generally include requirements for a well-defined body of scholarly knowledge;

completion of some standardized and prescribed course of study; examination and certification by a state and oversight by a state agency which has disciplinary powers over practitioners' behaviours. Parsons (2004, p. 15) claims the Global Alliance for Public Relations and Communication Management, of which the Institute of Public Relations, the Canadian Public Relations Society and the PRSA among others are members, has made assertions on the topic. It states that a profession is distinguished by specific characteristics, including 'master of a particular intellectual skill through education and training, acceptance of duties to a broader society than merely one's clients/employers, objectivity [and] high standards of conduct and performance.' It is the last tenet that places professional ethics squarely in the domain of defining a profession.

Sager (as cited in Sha, 2011, p. 121) distinguishes professions from simple trades in that the former require specialized knowledge, continuing education, codes of ethical conduct and the ability to enforce those codes (i.e. accountability). Based on previous research conducted on professionalism, Sha (2011, p. 121) claims that the characteristics of a profession include standardized education grounded in a theory-based body of knowledge, professional associations, codes of ethics, accountability and public recognition, as well as accreditation or certification.

Li et al. (2012) constructed their research based on previous studies conducted on the professionalism of public relations, and they studied six dimensions of perceived professional standards as follows:

- Role and function of PR in organizational strategic planning
- Sufficiency in personal training and preparedness
- Gender and racial equity
- Situational constraints
- Licensing and organizational support
- Participation in organizational decision-making teams

Six dimensions and items within these dimensions are analysed through the lenses of Turkish PR presidents of IPRA with an historical perspective and taking political economy of the times, both locally and globally.

Role and function of PR in organizational strategic planning

Research and measurement

According to Li et al. (2012), an effective PR department/unit sets measurable objectives. Consequently, goal setting and development of strategies to meet those goals are important in everyday public relations practices (p. 708); thus, research and measurement are essential parts of the practice. However, research skills are usually a shortcoming for PR practitioners.

Watson (2012) commented that by the start of the 1990s, measurement and evaluation have become major professional and practice issues in many countries.

However, when Mardin became IPRA president, the Turkish PR industry was far from having a strategic understanding dependent on research and measurement. Measurement and evaluation issues began to be included on the profession's agenda from the mid-1990s onwards. However, organizations in Turkey were reluctant to include these items in their budgets because they still treated public relations as a vehicle to obtain quick results, just like advertising (Bıçakçı & Hürmeriç, 2014, p. 22).

Remembering the 1990s, Betûl Mardin (personal communication, June 2016) indicates that one of the most important things for her is her client's image, and she would secretly investigate her client's image on their stakeholders. For instance, besides asking the opinion of her client's union representative, she would also ask the opinions of the client's neighbours, such as a market employee or a taxi driver, in person. She mentions that this kind of research would last for weeks, and she underlines the companies would cover the research budget when it was necessary. She asserts that research studies in the 1990s were mostly limited to image and reputation analysis.

The number of Turkish PR practitioners becoming IPRA members increased during Betûl Mardin's presidency. Consequently, Turkish PR practitioners had the opportunity to enhance their relationships with the globalized world, observe PR practices worldwide and import them into Turkey. One senior public relations practitioner says: 'International membership opportunities provide us with innovation from other countries. Both IPRA and PRSA execute effective and accessible activities and thus we are inspired by the efforts from around the world' (Başağa, 2008, p. 108). PR executive Meral Saçkan (2007) also complains about the reluctance of clients to spend money on research and measurement. Another PR executive, Ali Saydam, mentions that 'Standards and measurement in the PR sector gained importance in the middle of 1990s. "How can PR be measured?" was a question for us to be asked'. Eventually, following the global trends of international companies being reflected by IPRA, issues such as standards and measurement were first brought to the agenda of the Turkish PR industry in 1997 (Bıçakçı & Hürmeriç, 2014, p. 262).

Ceyda Aydede states that in the first half of the 2000s, it was still impossible to say that institutions in Turkey set measurable objectives for themselves. 'Although there was scientific data, the practitioners had no tools to interpret and use these data for their PR strategies. We can't say they know how to use the scientific tools' (Ceyda Aydede, personal communication, April 2020).

According to Güngör, the world was not facing a significant economic problem and narrowing during the 2010s. She mentions 'The world was indeed a "Global village" and corporations were increasingly globalizing in those years'. Multinational corporations were investing in different countries. Both marketing PR and corporate PR gained momentum because of the increasing international marketing efforts. Research studies were usually conducted based on the PR needs of the corporations, and strategies were built on the research findings. Local corporations in Turkey, as well as in other countries, were not doing research in those years.

Aydede points out that the demolition of the Eastern Bloc has implications for the PR profession and its role:

> When I became President of IPRA, it was a time when PR was trying to be spread more horizontally than vertically. Recognition and acknowledgment of the profession was our priority rather than strategically developing the PR practices in the light of scientific data, because there were still shortcomings in the field.
>
> (Ceyda Aydede, personal communication, April 2020)

Aydede states that she has adopted a mission of showing Eastern Bloc countries that PR is not a method for propaganda but is two-way communication. She has contributed to the establishment of PR departments in Bulgaria, Romania and Latvia and worked in Azerbaijan, which is also an ex-communist country. She has also organized a PR conference in Tehran, Iran, for the first time in the country's history. Aydede received PRSA's Atlas Award for Lifetime Achievement in International Public Relations in 2008. She was given this award for her extraordinary contributions to the practice and profession of public relations in an international environment over the span of her career (www.prsa.org/conferences-and-awards/awards/individual-awards/atlas-award).

Access to top management

Another dimension is that a practitioner should have direct access to top management, such as the President or CEO. However, Mardin complained this was not easy in the 1990s because 'The managers never had time for [them], they were always in a hustle, traveling continuously to abroad, to Europe. We were striving to reach them ...' (Personal communication, June 2016). Seeing public relations managers having access to company boards was a very distant dream for the public relations practitioners of that time. However, Güngör claims that PR practitioners could reach upper management directly and easily during the 2010s. Although most PR managers were operating under marketing departments, they were directly reporting to their CEOs or general managers.

Adaptation of professional ethics codes

Considering the role and power of public relations in terms of influencing public opinion, public relations practitioners are expected to behave ethically and take the interests of both their corporations and the public into account. As social trends of the past quarter of the twentieth century have resulted in the need for more strategic communication between organizations and their publics, there has been a concomitant increasing focus on the ethical behaviour of those organizations. As the interface between the organization and its public and, arguably, the keeper of the organizational reputation, the public relations function has an even more important role as the social conscience of the organization (Parsons, 2004, p. 12).

Hence, a number of studies point out that the public relations profession should serve as the conscience of corporations (Heath, 2004; Fitzpatrick & Bronstein, 2006; Bowen, 2008; Hürmeriç, 2016; Tindall et al., 2017).

In 1950, the PRSA adopted its first Code of Ethics in order to provide guidance for its members exercising ethical behaviour in the field. This was followed by the Code of Venice in 1961 and of Athens, Greece on May 12, 1965 when the IPRA adopted a draft of an International Code of Ethics for public relations practice. Watson (2014, p. 707) states that most public relations professional bodies and trade associations, such as the Chartered Institute of Public Relations (CIPR) and the Public Relations Consultants Association (PRCA) in the United Kingdom, also have some form of ethical rules or codes.

In Turkey, there are two associations that deal with the public relations ethics. The Public Relations Association of Turkey (TÜHİD) that was founded in 1972 is the first association, which gathers public relations professionals under the same roof. TÜHİD has launched the 12-item Code of Ethics launched to be applied by its members at both corporate and individual levels. The second association, The Communication Consultancies Association of Turkey (İDA), which was founded in 2004, is the local representative of International Communications Consultancy Organization (ICCO) (Hürmeriç & Ülger, 2015). The Code of Ethics launched by İDA is prepared based on the ethics principles of the associations IPR, IPRA, CERP and ICCO (İDA, 2020).

Three women presidents of IPRA were asked about adoption of professional ethics codes during their presidencies. Turkey scores exceptionally poorly with respect to its business/private-sector corruption (Koç, 2006, p. 333). Mardin says that the disputes were usually about bribery; despite facilitation payments and gifts being illegal, they were frequently encountered by the companies:

> Bribery was considered too dangerous. Extramarital relations were also important both abroad and in Turkey as significant factors that influenced reputation. The code of ethics was one of the first things to appear.
> (Betûl Mardin, personal communication, June 2016)

Nonetheless, Aydede claims professional ethical principles in PR were unknown in the 2000s. She says:

> I struggled a lot in terms of this subject. My colleagues accused me of being an old fogy during my personal struggle because, at the time, I was arguing that it wasn't right to work with more than one client from the same industry. Today, the situation is different but, at those times, the strategies were hidden and we were careful not to disclose the strategies to competitors. We translated ethical codes into our language, tried to spread them, but I can't say they are applied sufficiently. There was a particular '*zakazukha*' incident. If some money was paid while sending the press

release, the bulletin would be published without any questioning, like an ad text. A Russian PR agency, which wants to decipher this situation, sent a press release about the launch of a shop that does not actually exist and they paid to the newspaper; subsequently, this fake news was published! That is not how it happened in Turkey but we all experienced an incident in Russia together at that time.

(Ceyda Aydede, personal communication, April 2020)

Media non-transparency has also been known as cash for news coverage (Kruckeberg & Tsetsura, 2003), media bribery (Tsetsura, 2005b), envelope journalism (Shafer, 1990), paid news (Tsetsura & Zuo, 2009) and media opacity; non-transparent practices exist all over the world (cited in Tsetsura, 2011b, p. 172). Many practitioners use slang words to refer to this phenomenon: *zakazukha* is the name in Russian (Holmes, 2001, cited in Tsetsura, 2011b, p. 173). Even Aydede refrains from saying so; ethical issues regarding public relations and media relations were not so bright in Turkey. Koç (2006) investigates potential incidences of publishing custom-made news stories and editorials by newspapers and magazines about Turkish and international businesses for promoting their advertising space. Koç finds that the incidence of corresponding news stories or editorials in newspapers and magazines and related paid advertisements increased by more than 100% between 1994 and 2004 (p. 331).

Aydede also conveys her impressions about journalists who make news in exchange for money, and she narrates one of her research attempts with results that were unable to be published:

Through 2001–2002, in IPRA, we made a study on the *zakazukha* case, (with a University in America, but she does not remember the name). In fact, the sponsor of this study was the Hürriyet newspaper (flagship of the Turkish print press). The results of the study came to Turkey. When the findings were to be written, the editor-in-chief at that time prevented them from being published because he did not find them in compliance with his own approach. However, the newspaper's boss had already allocated a $10,000 budget to this scientific study in which data was collected from all over the world on such an international scale. According to this study, whose results were never published, Turkey came out somewhere in the middle rank and Norway was the most successful country in terms of ethics.

(Ceyda Aydede, personal communication, April 2020)

Concerning media and PR ethics, Aydede mentioned that the issue of racism in America was more prominent, and black people were experiencing discrimination where some newspapers were demanding money to publish stories of black people. She also remarked:

PR employees' relationships with journalists were the biggest ethical problem, as the relationships were not transparent. Here, the customer's ethical understanding comes into play and demands can sometimes have unethical consequences. I had to respond to the media's demands too.

(Ceyda Aydede, personal communication, April 2020)

According to Güngör, although PR professionals were indeed aware of the ethical codes of PR, it was still hard to generalize about the adaptation of these codes. She claims that while some corporations were meticulous about the ethical implications of their practices; some corporations did not give enough importance to codes of ethics.

Coombs and Holladay (2014, p. 25) underline that while most countries have some form of public relations association, it is a commonplace for only a minority of practitioners to belong to a professional organization and to be subject to its codes of conduct or ethics.

Sufficiency in professional training and preparedness

Formal education and necessary skills

As a dimension of professional standards, a liberal arts degree is considered appropriate training for public relations (Li et al., 2012). In Turkey, there was an evolution in higher education regarding Public Relations in 1992; all the journalism schools, under which public relations education was already established, now could offer a four-year Public Relations degree programme (Okay & Okay, 2008). Although Public Relations education had started then, the graduates were absent in the field until the new millennium. Betûl Mardin mentioned that most practitioners who had various academic backgrounds, primarily law, were trained internally, and the company had been like an academy for new practitioners.

As an industrial engineer, Aydede thinks that analytical capabilities are extremely important for PR professionals; however, PR graduates hardly had those skills:

> I was very surprised and upset for the lack of mathematics education and the inadequacy of statistical education in the communication faculties. That's why I did not prefer to employ communication faculty graduates, so I have been harshly criticized in the association (HiD, *Halkla İlişkiler Derneği* Turkish Public Relations Association, today named as 'TÜHİD'). I preferred graduates of departments, which include statistical education, such as psychology and sociology. Since they don't know how to do this, they are not able to be scientific and work based on scientific research. This is not a choice. I've tried to overcome this obstacle. I have acted this way because I do not prefer PR activities that are based on subjective assessments.

(Ceyda Aydede, personal communication, April 2020)

The prescriptive model for public relations education, formulated by IPRA and known as 'The Wheel of Education', was proposed to suggest generally accepted educational standards. The model takes the form of a recommended curriculum accompanied by a set of general recommendations pertaining to education and research (Ferreira, 1997). When considering public relations education in Turkey, it is seen that it is in line with the basic training programme of eight items proposed for public relations education in IPRA's Fourth Book of the Golden Book Series (Canpolat, 2012). However, Aydede does not think that the education, albeit in line with the formula proposed by her own association, is sufficient.

As the Internet was introduced in Turkey in 1993 in co-operation with The Scientific and Technological Research Council of Turkey and the Middle East Technical University for academic and scientific use (Geray, 1999), Aydede mentions that the Internet was already in their lives in the 2000s, even though social media was not. Therefore, it was important that PR employees had technological skills, but, according to her, the most important skill was still empathy and the ability to perceive and analyse the other person correctly.

Li et al. (2012, p. 708) found that 'intuition is a major part of decision-making in PR', and Betûl Mardin talked about the importance of her motto 'tolerance' while the other two IPRA presidents accentuated 'empathy'. Therefore, one can claim that not only formal education but also an ability to perceive people and society has always been crucial for standardization in PR practice.

Regarding the educational background of public relations professionals, Güngör claims, 'Although it can be said that most PR practitioners had received a PR education, a big percentage of PR practitioners graduated from other fields of social sciences, such as marketing and sociology. Additionally, a significant number of ex-journalists were changing their field and starting to work in the PR sector' (personal communication, April 2020).

Social responsibilities

In recent decades, consumers and other activists, including shareholders, have called for corporations to be more socially responsible. Hence, interest has grown in the concept Corporate Social Responsibility, especially since 2000 when the Global Compact was founded by the then UN Secretary General, Kofi Annan. Environmental concerns and that of marginalized publics (e.g. social justice movements) have likewise been included (Sriramesh & Duhé, 2009).

Aydede says that her company, named Global, is one of the first companies to sign the Global Compact in Turkey. She states that she has represented her company in the Global Compact meetings in Paris, Shanghai and the United States and has learned a lot about the concept of social responsibility. She states that in those years, many of their customers have been informed about this issue, and they have put a clause in their annual plans for making them a member of the Global Compact. Therefore, she says they were leading them to sign the deal. Aydede believes that a practitioner's function is not just a job but also performing as a public service to the community:

> There was a green book I was trying to implement in my own company. With an application called 'Green Global', we tried to fulfil our environmental

responsibilities within the company. I believe in essence before communication. We set an example for others by doing Global Compact reporting but the concept of CSR evolved over time and began to be understood differently. It was reduced to activities that were carried out just for the sake of announcement, instead of the required activities. Turkcell has a social responsibility project called 'Kardelenler' (Snowdrops). They spent 10 times more money to promote the project, compared to the money they spent on the program.

The project 'Kardelenler' was a social responsibility project initiated by Turkcell, one of the leading GSM operators in Turkey, in collaboration with the Association for Supporting Contemporary Life (Çağdaş Yaşamı Destekleme Derneği). The project started in the year 2000 with giving educational scholarships to 5000 girls who were economically disadvantaged and willing to pursue their education. The project was expanded in 2007 and 10,000 girls across Turkey received a scholarship each year. In ten years, 9,634 girls graduated from high school, 3,437 girls started their undergraduate education and 976 girls graduated from the university. The project won 16 national and international awards (http://yatirimci.turkcell.com.tr/2010/daha-fazla-sosyal-sorumluluk/kardelenlerb944.html?o=DahaFazlaSosyalAlt01&osa=dfs01).

When the 2000s arrived, new regulations in the area of cultural policies were initiated in Turkey. Meanwhile, the EU membership process has also been influential. The government was also quite encouraging for the private sector to invest more in cultural activities through its regulations (İnce, 2009). Aydede suggests that this situation has repercussions in the PR sector, but she also mentions that there are faulty perspectives in that area. She emphasizes a dominant approach: 'Promoting is the priority, then comes doing a good job', and she complains 'A good job already promotes itself. I don't think I am good at explaining it. We trained our staff but unfortunately it was not possible to train customers...' (Ceyda Aydede, personal communication, April 2020).

Gender and racial equity

According to the standards for PR practice and regardless of race and gender, everyone should be paid the same (Li et al., 2012, pp. 707–708).

Mardin states that in the 1990s, prejudices were exhibited because she was a woman, a Turk and a Muslim. She could speak English as well as her mother tongue, and she knew sufficient French to understand it, which made it easier for them to accept her. Even her European outlook has had an effect on breaking down the prejudices.

Although there is male dominance in the PR industry around the world, women started to get stronger in my time. Every time I spoke, I always talked about the power of women. I was saying that I was proud during official IPRA speeches (Betûl Mardin, personal communication, June 2016).

Aydede remarks that neither her company nor her customers have a gender-based fee policy and comments on gender issues as follows:

> I remember that PR executives were always men at international meetings back in the day. It is an industry where gender and racial discrimination shouldn't be made. However, in the early years of the 2000s, African-American employees were very few at international corporate conferences. In the period up to 2010, I've seen them more represented in the field. In Turkey, the PR sector was mainly predominated by women. However, with male journalists who were unemployed after the 2001 economic crisis, a gender balance in the sector was established.
> (Ceyda Aydede, personal communication, April 2020)

Güngör (personal communication, April 2020), argues that although PR practitioners in Europe were generally men in the 2010s, it was the opposite in Turkey. The number of women PR practitioners exceeded the number of men in the field. She also emphasizes that she has never encountered gender discrimination in the profession in Turkey or in Europe.

Situational constraints

A major situational constraint is that management perceives the public relations role as being more of a technician than a manager (Li et al., 2012). Even though the role of public relations professionals began to evolve slightly from that of a technician to a strategic partner during the 1990s (Bıçakçı & Hürmeriç, 2014, p. 11), Mardin mentions that most enterprise managers were still not aware of the real meaning of PR. She states that:

> They mostly misunderstood the concept of PR and they expected a more direct tool to increase the sales, such as advertising. It was a real challenge for us to express that this profession was all about image and reputation of the company. They were still asking about why the profits did not improve that month!
> (Betûl Mardin, personal communication, June 2016)

In her analysis of the contemporary profession, she points out that the image of the term 'public relations' is directly related with the very own image of the PR professional. Mardin, being a PR expert in her 60s, benefits from the advantages of her maturity in this context.

According to Aydede, companies often understood the necessity of PR after experiencing a crisis. 'At some point, the PR suddenly became popular, it flourished, moved to the top positions. Between 2003 and 2005, executive staff were particularly lacking'. However, a public relations department was generally too busy putting out fires, like a crisis, to develop a long-term strategic plan, she concludes (Ceyda Aydede, personal communication, April 2020).

Güngör also claims that both in local and international corporations, PR practitioners were generally perceived as technicians. The only exception was when the PR practitioner was not solely responsible for PR but also responsible for the strategic planning of all communications management, including advertising. Those practitioners were perceived as and had job titles as managers. Unfortunately, executives used to underestimate the PR profession as they thought PR is a practice that can easily be done by everyone. We should criticize ourselves and accept that as PR practitioners, we were not able to explain our profession well enough (Zehra Güngör, personal communication, April 2020).

Licensing and organizational support

Public relations should be a licensed profession (Li et al. 2012, p. 708). Mardin recalls the 1990s and says, 'Most of the meetings we had in IPRA at that time were about defining the rules of PR as a profession and about its accreditation. There were always discussions about professional organization' (Betûl Mardin, personal communication, June 2016).

Aydede talks about the difficulty of establishing international standards in PR and the competition between associations; she narrates one of the highest spots in her career:

> PRSA has a certification program; I joined it. I finally took the oral exam and I passed it. However the management team of IPRA, who were aware of my attempt, was disturbed. They called me and said that IPRA already had its own standards and they were more important; there was no need for another standard. Because of the pressure, I gave up the written exam and, therefore, PRSA's certificate. So, it is possible to say that the standards in the sector are not uniform and that each group produces its own standards.
> (Ceyda Aydede, personal communication, April 2020)

Güngör underlines the importance of licensing and organizational support for public relations and explains the efforts in the 2010s as organizing international conferences and congresses in order to emphasize the value and importance of public relations. She also asserts that notable associations today are carrying on these efforts. She also noted that she took serious steps in order to establish a chapter in IPRA, consisting of Turkic Republics (Azerbaijan, Kazakhstan, Kyrgyzstan, Turkmenistan), Georgia and Turkey. Today, it is still in progress. She also visited Iran and West African countries and gave speeches about her professional experiences (Zehra Güngör, personal communication, April 2020).

Participation in organizational decision-making teams

In the 1990s, public relations professionals were far from being a part of the managerial team and by the end of the decade, they still had difficulty in assuming a more prominent role in clients' decision-making processes (Bıçakçı & Hürmeriç, 2014, p. 263).

According to Aydede, PR executives were not on the boards of directors at the beginning of the new millennium. Here is how she summarizes how they did business in those days:

> We went through a process like this: PR was perceived as work that women used to do in our country at first. With the Özal period and international expansion, with the arrival of foreign companies into the country, there were expectations from PR departments here in line with the changing wishes and needs. Therefore, it turned out that different features were needed for PR and the senior management of such companies began to put slightly more talented people in charge of these departments randomly. However, these people did not have sufficient knowledge, which they needed for the practice but this was now an executive position and they became very loyal employees to maintain their positions because they were in an administrative position and did not have sufficient professional background. They approved everything the senior manager said and, because they did not have the skills of the position they undertook, they began to pass on the manager's requests to the agencies without filtering them, without their own personal ideas. At the points we opposed them, there was a barrier between us in terms of communication because they didn't understand us and didn't have the courage to escalate criticisms to the management. When it was requested to access senior administration directly, the internal department had to be bypassed and the effort to reach management in different, strange ways appeared under obligation. This disturbing situation has prevented the progress of the sector.
> (Ceyda Aydede, personal communication, April 2020)

According to Güngör, PR practitioners in Turkey did not have a role in the decision-making process of corporations. Very few of the PR practitioners in international corporations were actively involved in the decision-making process (Zehra Güngör, personal communication, April 2020).

Conclusion

This chapter aimed to reveal the progressive elaboration of public relations practice from the perspectives of three Turkish women IPRA presidents within three decades (1990s, 2000s and 2010s). Public relations is a profession strongly influenced by social, cultural, political, economic and technological improvements around the world. As a profession, there is an ongoing debate about the standards of public relations. PR scholars have investigated the role of public relations practitioners, examined the codes of conduct, gender differences, professional bodies of work and associations in various studies. In this study, six dimensions of professional standards were analysed through the perspectives of three Turkish women IPRA presidents. Betül Mardin, Ceyda

Aydede and Zehra Güngör, they all emphasized that public relations has been constantly evolving both in Turkey and in the world during their presidencies. Hence, there have been significant developments regarding the dimensions analysed in this chapter. There is no doubt that all three Turkish women IPRA presidents have contributed to the public relations field in their efforts of raising the professional standards. As the findings are limited to the framework created by the oral representation of three women practitioner's memoirs, they give us an understanding about their perceptions and priorities as directors of an international PR association.

References

Başağa, A. (2008). Besteyle Güftenin Örtüşmediği bir Sosyal Sorumluluk Projesi olmaz (There cannot be a social responsibility project where the lyrics do not synchronize with the composition). In F. Balta Peltekoğlu and A. Saydam (Eds.) *Sektörün Penceresinden Halkla İlişkiler (Public Relations from the Vantage point of the Industry)*, Istanbul: Propedia Yayıncılık. pp. 79–112.

Bıçakçı, A. B. and Hürmeriç, P. (2013). Milestones in Turkish public relations history, *Public Relations Review*, 39(2), 91–100.

Bıçakçı, A. B. and Hürmeriç, P. (2014) *The Historical Development of Public Relations Profession in Turkey: The Rise of a Profession in Times of Social Transformation*. In Burton St. J. III, Lamme M. O., L'Etang J., (Eds.) *Pathways to Public Relations: Histories of Practice and Profession*, Oxon: Routledge. pp. 257–272.

Broom, G. M. (1982). A Comparison of Sex Roles in Public Relations, *Public Relations Review*, 8 (3), 17–22.

Cameron, G. T., Sallot, L. M. and Weaver Lariscy, R. A. (1996). Developing standards of professional performance in public relations, *Public Relations Review*, 22 (1), 43–61.

Canpolat, N. (2012). *Geçmişten Günümüze Örneklerle Türkiye'de Halkla İlişkiler'in Gelişimi (From past to the present: The development of Public Relations in Turkey with examples)*, Ankara: Seçkin.

Creedon, P. J. (2011). Public Relations and "Women's Work": Toward a Feminist Analysis of Public Relations Roles, In Grunig, L. A and Grunig, J. E., (Eds.) *Public Relations Research Annual 3*, Hillsdale, NJ, Lawrence Erlbaum and Assoc., pp. 67–84.

Daymon, C. and Demetrious, K. (2010). Gender and public relations: Perspectives, applications and questions. PRism 7(4): www.prismjournal.org.

Fitch, K., James, M. and Motion J. (2016). Talking back: Reflecting on feminism, public relations and research, *Public Relations Review*, 42, 279–287.

Geray, H. (1999). Network policy formation between idealist and strategic models: a political economy perspective from Turkey, *Telecommunications Policy*, 23, 495–511.

Hürmeriç, P. (2016). Public Relations and Ethics: An Ongoing Debate (Halkla İlişkiler ve Etik: Süregiden Tartışma), In Balta Peltekoğlu, F. (Ed.) *The Power of Communication: From Corporate to Global Public Relations (İletişimin Gücü: Kurumsaldan Küresele Halkla İlişkiler)*, Istanbul: Beta., pp. 407–434.

Hürmeriç, P. and Ülger, B. (2015). Ethics statements of public relations agencies in Turkey: How do Turkish PR agencies present themselves on the web? In Catellani, A., Zerfass, A., Tench, R. (Eds.). Communication Ethics in a Connected World: Research in Public Relations and Organizational Communication, Peter Lang., pp. 135–153.

İDA (2020, May 10). www.ida.org.tr/ornek-sayfa/meslek-ahlaki-ilkeleri/.

İnce, H. A. (2009). Yerel düzlemdeki kamu idareleri ve kültür politikaları. (Cultural politics and public management in local level), In S. Ada, and H. A. İnce (Eds.), *Türkiye'de kültür politikalarına giriş (Introduction to Cultural Politics in Turkey)*, İstanbul: İstanbul Bilgi Üniversitesi Yayınları, pp. 219–245.

Koç, E. (2006). "Order three advertisements and get one news story free": Public relations ethics practices of Turkish and international companies in Turkey, *Public Relations Review*, 32, 331–340.

Krider, D. S. and Ross, P. G. (1997). The experiences of women in a public relations firm: A phenomenological explication, *Journal of Business Communication*, 34(4), 437–454.

Lee, H., Place, K. R. and Smith, B. G. (2018). Revisiting gendered assumptions of practitioner power: An exploratory study examining the role of social media expertise, *Public Relations Review*, 44, 191–200.

Li, C., Cropp, F., Sims, W. and Jin, Y. (2012) Perceived professional standards and roles of public relations in China: Through the lens of Chinese public relations practitioners, *Public Relations Review*, 38, 704–710.

Mellado, C. and Barría, S. (2012). Development of professional roles in the practice of public relations in Chile, *Public Relations Review*, 38, 446–453.

Okay, A. and Okay, A. (2008). Undergraduate and graduate Public Relations Education in Turkey: A quantitative study of dissertations' contributions to public relations field (1984–2007), *Selçuk İletişim*, January, 5–14.

Öksüz, B. and Görpe, S. (2014). Woman's place in the field of public relations in Turkey: Perspectives of academics, practitioners, and representatives of professional organizations on it, *İstanbul Üniversitesi İletişim Fakültesi Dergisi (Journal of İstanbul University, Faculty of Communication)*, 2(47), 125–142.

Place, K. R. (2012). Power-control or empowerment? How women public relations practitioners make meaning of power, *Journal of Public Relations Research*, 24, 435–450.

Sha, B. (2011). Accredited vs. non-accredited: The polarization of practitioners in the public relations profession, *Public Relations Review*, 37, 121–128.

Siler, M. N. (2009). *Telling the story of women's contributions to public relations: A content analysis of three public relations industry publications, 2001–2005*. (Unpublished MA dissertation). Ball State University, Indiana.

Sriramesh, K. (2003). Introduction, in Sriramesh, K. and Vercic D. (Ed) *The Global Public Relations Handbook*. Lawrence Erlbaum Associates, Publishers, London, pp. xxix.

Sriramesh, K. and Duhé, S.C. (2009). Extending cultural horizons: Political economy and public relations, *Public Relations Review*, 23, 368–375.

Tench, R. and Topić, M. (2017). One step forward, two steps back? An analysis of European PR practitioners' views on the position of women in the PR industry (2009–2015), *Current Politics and Economics of Europe*, 28(1), 83–105.

Toth, E. L. and Grunig, L. A. (1993). The missing story of women in public relations, *Journal of Public Relations Research*, 5(3), 153–175.

Tsetsura, K. (2011a). Is public relations a real job? How female practitioners construct the profession, *Journal of Public Relations Research*, 23(1), 1–23.

Tsetsura, K. (2011b). Cultural and historical aspects of media transparency in Russia, In Nikolev, A. G. (Ed.) *Ethical Issues in International Communication*, London: Palgrave Macmillan, pp. 172–182.

Watson, T. (2012). The evolution of public relations measurement and evaluation. *Public Relations Review*, 38(3), 390–398.

Watson, T. (2014). IPRA Code of Athens—The first international code of public relations ethics: Its development and implementation since 1965, *Public Relations Review*, 40(4), 707–714.

Wrigley, B. J. (2002). Glass ceiling? What glass ceiling? A qualitative study of how women view the glass ceiling in public relations and communications management, *Journal of Public Relations Research*, 14(1), 27–55.

Yaxley, H. M. L. (2013). Career experiences of women in British public relations, *Public Relations Review*, 39, 156–165.

TURKCELL, (2020, April 14) http://yatirimci.turkcell.com.tr/2010/daha-fazla-sosyal-sorumluluk/kardelenlerb944.html?o=DahaFazlaSosyalAlt01&osa=dfs01

5 Betty Stewart, Orientalism and *Oriental Cavalcade*
Entertainment public relations in late 1950s Australia

Kate Fitch

Introduction

This chapter emerges from a larger biographical project investigating Betty Stewart's six-decade career in public relations in Australia. Although Stewart (2000, 2004) maintained she started the third public relations agency in Australia and recognised she was a contemporary of Eric White,[1] her story is not recorded in Australian public relations history. In this chapter, I focus on 1959, when Stewart, at the age of 44, left the Tivoli Theatre Circuit after almost three decades working in theatres to pursue her 'dream' of running her own public relations company. Her first client, theatrical entrepreneur Tibor Rudas, retained her to work on his Tivoli show *Oriental Cavalcade*, and Stewart spent the next six months promoting the show in Melbourne, Sydney and Brisbane. This campaign allowed her to establish her own consultancy. Stewart's self-published memoir, *A Survivor in a Star Spangled World*, an oral history in the National Library, along with her donation of 38 boxes of notebooks, correspondence, photographs, press cuttings and souvenirs to the Australian Performing Arts Collection, suggests Stewart was keen to have her achievements recognised. I acknowledge Stewart's hand in collating and preparing her archives for staged donations to the Australian Performing Arts Collection, and that this poses some historiographical challenges. In this chapter, therefore, I seek to triangulate different sources of data, drawing on the oral history, self-published memoirs, the Betty Stewart Collection, digitised newspapers and secondary sources.

Despite the flourishing interest in public relations history in the last decade, very little has been written about female practitioners and their contributions to the historical development of the field. The aim of this chapter, then, is to investigate an Australian female public relations 'pioneer' who established a consultancy in the late 1950s; the focus is on her first campaign as a consultant. The campaign is significant in that it enabled Stewart to establish her business in a decade that saw the growing professionalisation of public relations and relates to an understudied sector. First, I introduce Stewart and briefly outline her career, which began in theatres in the early 1930s. Following the establishment of Betty Stewart Enterprises in 1959, Stewart's client list expanded beyond entertainment public relations to include shopping centres, cruise ships, television programmes, sports competitions and international brands such as Revlon and Weightwatchers; her career ended only with her retirement in the early 1990s. Second, I investigate the promotion of *Oriental Cavalcade*, a show that featured performers from various countries in Asia alongside English, American and Australian performers. This investigation enables insights into routine public relations work in the entertainment sector at that time. Third, in the final section, I consider the significance of Stewart's promotional strategy for *Oriental Cavalcade*, focusing on Orientalist and 'exotic Asian' tropes. To conclude, I identify the factors contributing to the exclusion of certain kinds of public relations work, such as entertainment public relations, from gendered professional conceptualisations of the field.

Betty Stewart Enterprises

Stewart left school at 14 to attend business college and then began working as a secretarial assistant to the publicity director at J. C. Williamson Theatres in the early 1930s. She left upon getting married but returned in a more senior role during the war, describing theatre as 'vital' to the war effort (Stewart, 2004). Stewart continued to work in theatres, twice leaving to travel to England, where she worked in magazine advertising. On her return to Australia in 1954, she briefly worked in advertising, which she hated, and began working for the Tivoli Theatre Circuit later that year. As Tivoli historian van Straten writes, vaudeville theatre was 'chorus girls, legs, comics and lots of noise' (2003: 200). In 1959, Stewart left the Tivoli. One reason may have been the sudden death of joint managing director, David N. Martin, in 1958, which resulted in his son, Lloyd Martin, taking over the Tivoli (Rutledge, 2000; van Straten, 2003); there is at least one terse memo from L. Martin to Stewart asking to be updated on her publicity efforts. According to Stewart (2004), 'a lot of the soul of the Tivoli went' following D. Martin's death.

Stewart offers various reasons for her decision to leave the Tivoli and establish her consultancy. In her oral history interview, Stewart (2004) initially says 'it happened' but when pressed for a fuller response, said 'I felt the bottom was falling out of it'. As Stewart acknowledged, the Tivoli audiences dwindled in response to the introduction of television in Australia in July 1956, a problem for many commercial theatres; however, the first Melbourne television show was broadcast live from the Tivoli in November that year, and Tivoli performances featured in regular Sunday night broadcasts (Cox, 2006; van Straten, 2003). Stewart, as publicity director at the Tivoli, therefore had early experience of booking performers for, and working with, television studios and often integrated television appearances into her publicity campaigns.

Stewart's (2000, 2004) accounts of how she gained her first client, Tibor Rudas and his Tivoli variety show *Oriental Cavalcade*, do not match the evidence in the archives. Stewart (2004) said in her oral history that Tibor Rudas 'rang me up and he said, "Oh, you've got to come back." And I said, "Oh, I can't."

He said, "Well, I'll be your first client."' In the book, Stewart offers a different version:

> When he [Tibor Rudas] heard he was not going to have my services, he really was mad and stormed into my office demanding that I must stay. When this had no effect, he then amazed me by saying if I was not going to stay on at the Tivoli, he would be the first client in my new business. He made me an offer on a weekly retainer that was about four times what I was getting at the Tivoli.
>
> (Stewart, 2000: 110)

However, in a letter in the archives from Stewart to Rudas dated 29 June 1959, Stewart informs him of her resignation and offers her services as a consultant, as she had already begun working on the promotion for *Oriental Cavalcade*.[2] It is possible this letter resulted from an initial discussion with Rudas, but the different retrospective accounts point to the unreliability of first person narratives (Fitch, 2015). Stewart (2000, 2004) recognises that establishing her own public relations agency was of historical significance in that there were few public relations companies at that time. However, as 'the only Public Relations Company with show business experience', Stewart was able to draw on show business clients to establish her consultancy (2000: 116). Stewart (2004) maintained:

> I had all the contacts. And I thought, I'll start my own business. Everyone was against it. I was the third PR company to start in Australia. ... I borrowed ... $250 from the bank manager and bought myself a typewriter and a few other things, and set up in my dining room in St Kilda Road.

Stewart initially worked out of the Tivoli office in Melbourne but also travelled to Sydney and Brisbane; however, Stewart (2000, 2004) was keen to return to Melbourne and develop her business.

Oriental Cavalcade *promotion*

Although *Oriental Cavalcade* was promoted as an exotic show from the East, many cast members were from England, Australia and the United States. The Rudas dancers were a professional Australian troupe, and the Tivoli ballet, 'the living golden goddesses', comprised 'blondes and redheads only'.[3] The headline act, Freddie Sales, was a British comedian (replaced by Tivoli regular, Will Mahoney in Brisbane) and the compere was American Billy Rayes. Other performers were Australian entertainer Johnny Lockwood, Australian tap dancer Billy McMahon and Australian acrobatic act Duo Sylvanos. Nevertheless, the 'lure of the orient' was the foremost framing in the promotional work for *Oriental Cavalcade*. 'What is the difference between East and West?' reads the promotional copy in one brochure, promising '12 sensational variety acts direct from the Orient'; 'gorgeous girls from 6 countries'; and 'the mystery of Siam, the fascination of China, the excitement of Malaya, the enchantment of India'.[4]

The performers from across Asia, apparently 'discovered' by Rudas who had successfully toured his dance troupe in the previous two years, included the Kawashima Girls, dancers from Japan (in fact, one was from Korea but had a Japanese stage name; and at least one news story suggested two of the dancers were Chinese [She'll get more fans, 1959]). In addition, there were Hong Kong jugglers and fire artists, Che Chung Chong and Mana Koon; Thai kick boxers Sawong and Thavil; Filipinos Don Soriano ('the Elvis of Manila'); the Ricman Duo, boy singers Ricardo Quiambao ('Ric'), aged 12, and German Zapanta ('Herman'), aged 14; and a rock 'n' roll band, Vic Solidad and the Blue Squire Trio. It is worth noting that the spelling of the names of these performers varied across different promotional materials (e.g. the Ricman Duo were also Ricmand and Ricmano, and Mana Koon was sometimes Mala).

Drawing on the material in the Betty Stewart Collection, including detailed memos and letters from Stewart to Rudas where she provided updates on the promotional activity, Stewart's role was primarily press liaison. This work entailed creating content for good photographic and editorial opportunities, building on her longstanding media contacts and understanding of media work. In a letter to one editor about her planned use of rickshaws to transport Japanese dancers on their arrival via train (which Stewart redubbed 'the Orient Express') in Sydney, Stewart writes: 'Tell your photographer to meet me and I'll see he gets the photos he wants'.[5] Stewart's role extended to writing paragraphs for newspaper columns; working closely with Harry Jay, Tivoli photographer, for publicity photos; managing the gala opening and backstage party; booking the performers on television such as HSV 7's new revue show, 'Bandwagon'; and organising press receptions. Stewart requested the Professional Musicians Club cater for approximately 150 people 'with savouries including cocktail sausages, oyster patties, party pies, sandwiches and liquor (beer, gin, whiskey)' for the press reception in Sydney.[6] Stewart exploited every opportunity, issuing media alerts and writing letters to newspaper, picture and magazine editors. For example, the cast arrival in Melbourne included an airport procession in goggomobils with performers, including '8 beautiful Japanese girls' in 'traditional' dress to maximise photo opportunities and press coverage.

Much of Stewart's strategy revolved around the Kawashima dancers. Stewart was relentless and acknowledged that the Japanese performers were not happy with some of her choices. She located a rickshaw – the search for a rickshaw became a news story – and insisted the Japanese performers wore kimonos at all press opportunities. In her book, she acknowledged they found the rickshaw ride 'very rough' and 'hated' wearing the 'uncomfortable' kimonos (Stewart, 2000: 111, 114). Stewart (2004) expands in her oral history interview:

> I had to get a rickshaw because I wanted to do a promotion that every time they went out the poor dears had to put the kimono on and drive in this

damned [rickshaw] ... and they were the most uncomfortable thing. But that was the way I wanted publicity.

Beyond media relations, Stewart's role also included stakeholder engagement and cross-promotions. For example, an *Oriental Cavalcade*-themed week in Foy's department store entailed daily cast appearances, fashion parades and window displays to promote the show and a photography competition, featuring performers at Foy's, to launch a new Japanese camera.[7] Other promotional activity included an exhibition by the Thai fighters at a sports stadium; in-store cooking demonstrations to promote Sunbeam kitchen appliances with diverse members of the cast; Japanese dancers modelling Jantzen swimwear on an Australian beach; and Coca-Cola sponsorship, which supplied the performers with soft drinks for the entire season. Stewart organised a four-page supplement in the *Daily Telegraph*, for which she provided a list of potential advertisers as well as the copy, photography and all editorial content. She negotiated a car sponsorship for the lead male act (Freddie Sales in Sydney and Melbourne as well as Will Mahoney in Brisbane) and offered a nightly acknowledgement of the dealer at each show as well as other publicity. Stewart organised the press reception in each city and invited the Thai, Korean, Chinese and Japanese consul generals, along with the Lord Mayor, to the gala opening night in Melbourne in August 1959. She organised a performance at Pentridge Prison and ensured the media were present (In black and white, 1959).[8] Many of the activities demanded the cast participate in fundraising events such as supporting Miss Tivoli at the Victorian Racing Club; street appeals for the £15,000 Spastic Children's Appeal; and photo opportunities, such as the Japanese dancers with Stewart's Australian Rules football team, the Melbourne Football Club, nicknamed the Demons, to cross-promote the club's fundraising revue.

Promoting 'Asia' in Australia

'Asia' is integral to the Australian identity, yet it is a contested and homogenising term that shows little understanding of the different countries and diverse cultures within the region (Fitch, 2016a; Knight & Heazle, 2011; Walker & Sobocinska, 2012). Much of the media coverage for *Oriental Cavalcade* drew heavily on Stewart's promotional material: 'There are 35 Asiatics in the cast, including Filipinos, Japanese, Chinese, Siamese, Malayans and Thais. They will appear with 21 Asians and Europeans but the atmosphere will be Oriental'.[9] Despite the American, British and Australian performers playing lead roles in *Oriental Cavalcade*, the 'Asian' elements provided the promotional strategy, with references to, for example, special bamboo imported from the Philippines for the Filipino dance sequence, a lighting designer from Japan, and that most of the stage setting was made in Japan and Siam. One critic's response to the show was, however, damning: 'a review [sic] that has to try hard to remain even vaguely oriental. The Eastern performers have been very Westernised' (Oriental Cavalcade, 1959). The theme of 'authenticity' informs Stewart's retrospective accounts; she noted, for example, 'Tibor did not bring any dancers from Tokyo because they were too Westernised' (Stewart, 2000: 111). However, the promotional strategy built around authenticity did not always succeed. One journalist took four Kawashima dancers, Sumoko Takamoto, Sachiko Kawaguchi, Yoshiko Enami and Eiko Shimuzi, to a hair salon to have their hair done like 'geisha girls' and stated 'they didn't enjoy it a bit', noting that modern Japanese women tend to cut and style their hair short.[10]

In a discussion of the internationalisation of Australian culture, Bollen points to Stewart's work in promoting and commodifying 'Asia' for Australian audiences through the *Oriental Cavalcade* campaign:

> Rudas hired publicist Betty Stewart who booked advertisers for the program and arranged for performers from the show to appear on television to promote the Sydney season. The advertisers took advantage of the revue to cultivate Australian tastes for consuming Asian music, food and experiences on holidays. The program for the Sydney season carries advertisements for: The Sukiyaki Room at King's Cross, 'Australia's only Japanese restaurant;' Miss Kawashima's favourite recipe for fried rice, cooked with Australian-grown Sunwhite rice; a recording from RCA records of 'music for a Chinese dinner at home,' with Chinese recipes on the cover; and Qantas and BOAC, the two main airlines flying from Sydney to Manila, Singapore and Hong Kong.
> (Bollen, 2013a: 71)

Stewart liked using what she referred to as a 'gimmick', a hook to draw media attention and which might make a good photo opportunity and create a story. She devised a couple to promote *Oriental Cavalcade*, including a promotional, printed 'invitational' record with music and songs from the show and specially printed and folded paper fans as souvenirs.[11] The fans were given to female audience members at the gala opening by three 'Chinese' models recruited from the Elly Lucas School of Charm in Melbourne and six women from the Chinese Sports Association in Sydney to provide more photo opportunities for the press. These models had nothing to do with *Oriental Cavalcade* but featured in media alerts provided by Stewart and were included in media coverage: 'Beautiful Chinese girls in their national costume, the cheongsam, will be grouped around the foyer to hand presentation fans to women patrons'.[12]

Stewart drew on all the cast to provide, sometimes exclusive, carefully targeted angles for different media outlets. However, the Japanese performers appeared to dominate much of the coverage and campaign, building on the theme of exotic, feminised other (see Said, 1978), with Stewart's insistence on them wearing kimonos and the promotion centring on their beauty. Bollen (2013b) describes how the imagery used in much of the marketing of *Oriental Cavalcade* 'recycled the eroticised tropes of Orientalism', with confusing harem scenes and near naked women. One news story even stated the Japanese performers were 'all single and under 20' (She'll get more fans, 1959) and another used the headline 'Invasion from the Fair East' (Findlay, 1959). Stewart (2000, 2004) identified a few cultural clashes, claiming the girls objected to being called geisha girls and expressed concern that their costumes were too revealing. Other gimmicks played on the 'Asian' theme, with Stewart producing colourful press invitations to opening nights and backstage parties in the shape of Chinese lanterns. Not all of Stewart's promotional ideas came off. She wanted ikebana displays in the theatre foyer for the gala opening but was informed by the president of Ikebana International that 'such arrangements would be unsuitable insomuch as they are geared for the intimacy of a home and would not be exotic enough to enhance the theatre'.[13]

Conclusion

This chapter offers important insights into Australian public relations history, in that researching forgotten and marginalised campaigns and sectors, such as Stewart's work on *Oriental Cavalcade*, highlight gaps in that history. Although historical narratives of public relations tend to confine entertainment public relations, particularly publicity work and the circus press agent, to public relations' past (Tilson, 2017), how such work is marginalised historically from 'modern PR' deserves further investigation. Stewart's grounding in entertainment public relations did not mean that her later public relations work was confined to entertainment as she moved increasingly into lifestyle, sport, travel, retail and other sectors. The research presented in this chapter therefore offers an opportunity for rethinking public relations practices and history beyond corporate parameters and from a gender perspective.

The campaign to promote *Oriental Cavalcade* did not just reflect the zeitgeist but produced and perpetuated stereotypes around Asian cultures. However, it must be understood within the context of Australia's Anglo culture and geographical location in Asia and the growing internationalisation of Australia in the 1950s, as air routes opened up and television became more common (Bollen, 2013a). In addition, the commodification of performers is typical in entertainment public relations (Tilson, 2017). Promoting *Oriental Cavalcade* as the mysterious East drew on many Asian tropes, revealing much about the Australian post-war identity as a Western, Anglo-Celt nation despite (or perhaps because of) its close proximity to countries in Asia. These tropes frame the East as Exotic other, as mysterious and unknowable (Said, 1978). In particular, feminised, fetishised Asian women, as can be seen in Stewart's emphasis on beauty and national dress in communications prepared for the media, provided multiple opportunities for attracting media coverage. At times, Stewart deliberately sought to contrast Australia-Asia cultures, evident in the staged photo opportunities for the press, such as the kimono-clad Japanese dancers 'teaching' Melbourne Demons' footballers to use chopsticks (Demon Had to Learn, 1959; Demons Go Oriental, 1959). This commodification of entertainers as 'exotic Asians' was primarily the public relations strategy underpinning the campaign, in order to sell tickets and ensure a successful theatre season (and, in turn, the success of Betty Stewart Enterprises). Cultural clashes, including dancers' concerns over being referred to as geisha girls, simply became further material to provide to the media (Here Come the Geisha Girls, 1959).

Situating this particular campaign within public relations history raises questions as to why entertainment public relations is yet to feature in Australian histories. These histories offer a professional narrative founded on post-war activity and rely primarily on the perspectives and retrospective accounts of a small number of male practitioners associated with the founding of professional institutes and major consultancies (Fitch, 2016a). The professional drive ensured that corporate and government work, particularly associated with agencies such as Eric White Associates, were elevated, while publicity and promotional work in sectors such as entertainment with the taint of circus promotion haunting public relations' past were relegated to technical public relations and therefore excluded from historical accounts. This exclusion, as I have argued elsewhere, is typical of feminised work (Fitch, 2016b; Fitch & Third, 2010, 2014). Stewart's gender therefore contributes to her absence from twentieth-century Australian public relations history, despite her 60-year career.

Focusing on Stewart's first campaign as a consultant offers unique insights into routine public relations work in an understudied sector. These insights include an emphasis on expertise in media relations, and a corresponding capacity to develop and build on professional media networks, as well as the ability to undertake extensive cross promotion with the retail and charity sectors. This 1959 campaign coincides with the decade when state-based professional institutes and public relations consultancies emerged, as the industry sought professional legitimacy by demarcating itself as offering a unique service or expertise that differed from advertising (Fitch, 2016a; L'Etang, 2004). The fact that Stewart's decision to open a public relations consultancy, within a few years of Eric White Associates establishing an office in Melbourne (Griffen-Foley, 2012), is largely unheralded points to the urgent need for more 'herstories' in order to fully comprehend the historical development of public relations in Australia.

Acknowledgements

My thanks to Claudia Funder at the Australian Performing Arts Collection, Arts Centre Melbourne, and Fiona Milway at the National Library of Australia in Canberra for assistance in facilitating access to archival sources.

Notes

1 Eric White is a post-war pioneer of Australian public relations; by 1964, Eric White Associates was the first publicly listed public relations company in Australia, and one of the largest in the world with offices throughout Australia and Asia (Griffen-Foley, 2012; Sheehan, 2014).
2 Letter from Stewart to Tibor Rudas dated 29 June 1959. Betty Stewart Collection, 1999.060.453.
3 Tibor Rudas presents Oriental Cavalcade [four-page-folded promotional brochure]. Betty Stewart Collection, 1999.060.426.

4 Tibor Rudas presents Oriental Cavalcade [four-page-folded promotional brochure]. Betty Stewart Collection, 1999.060.426.
5 Letter from Stewart to Neal Kendrick, *The Sun* Pictorial Editor, Sydney, 6 October 1959. Betty Stewart Collection, 1999.060.455.
6 Letter from Stewart to Eric E. Cox, Secretary, Professional Musicians Club, 24 September 1959. Betty Stewart Collection, 1999.060.455.
7 Letter from Stewart to Tibor Rudas, 29 June 1959. Betty Stewart Collection, 1999.060.455.
8 Letter from Stewart to Mr. Palmer, *The Sun News-Pictorial*, Melbourne, 11 September 1959. Betty Stewart Collection, 1999.060.455.
9 Exotic and Lavish Show. (c. 1959). [press cutting, source unknown]. Betty Stewart Collection, 1999.060.452.
10 Breen, E. (c. 1959). Sayonara means goodbye [press cutting, source unknown]. Betty Stewart Collection, 1999.060.452.
11 Record cards for Oriental Cavalcade. Betty Stewart Collection, 2002.034.594; Souvenir fans for Oriental Cavalcade. Betty Stewart Collection, 2002.034.598.
12 Exotic and Lavish Show. [c. 1959, press cutting, source unknown]. Betty Stewart Collection, 1999.060.452.
13 Letter to Stewart from Mrs. Garrett, President of Ikebana International, 15 August 1959. Betty Stewart Collection, 1999.060.455.

References

Archival sources

Betty Stewart Collection. Australian Performing Arts Collection, Arts Centre Melbourne, Australia.
Stewart, B. (2004, August 16) [oral history recorded with Bill Stephens]. TRC 5191, National Library of Australia.

Non-archival sources

Bollen, J. (2013a). Here from there—travel, television and touring revues: Internationalism as entertainment in the 1950s and 1960s. *Popular Entertainment Studies*, 4(1), pp. 64–81.
Bollen, J. (2013b, July 25). Oriental Cavalcade. Research on performance and desire. Accessed 7 January 2020 from Jonathan Bollen.net.
Cox, P. (2006). *On the Box: Great Moments in Australian Television*. Sydney, Australia: Powerhouse Publishing.
Demons Go Oriental. (1959, August 14). *The Sun News-Pictorial*, p. 24.
Demon Had to Learn. (1959, August 14). *The Sun News-Pictorial*, p. 1.
Findlay, D. (1959, August 10). Invasion from the Fair East. *The Sun News-Pictorial*, p. 1.
Fitch, K. (2015). Making history: Reflections on memory and 'elite' interviews in public relations research. *Public Relations Inquiry*, 4(2), 131–144.
Fitch, K. (2016a). *Professionalizing Public Relations: History, Gender and Education*. London, England: Palgrave Macmillan.
Fitch, K. (2016b). Feminism and public relations. In J. L'Etang, D. McKie, N. Snow & J. Xifra (Eds.), *Routledge Handbook of Critical Public Relations* (pp. 54–64). London, England: Routledge.

Fitch, K. and Third, A. (2010). Working girls: Revisiting the gendering of public relations. *Prism*, 7(4). Accessed from www.prismjournal.org/uploads/1/2/5/6/125661607/v7-no4-a1.pdf.

Fitch, K. and Third, A. (2014). Ex-journos and promo girls: Feminization and professionalization in the Australian public relations industry. In C. Daymon and K. Demetrious (Eds.), *Gender and Public Relations: Critical Perspectives on Voice, Image and Identity* (pp. 247–268). London, England: Routledge.

Griffen-Foley, B. (2012). Eric White (1915–1989). *Australian Dictionary of Biography*. Accessed from http://adb.anu.edu.au/biography/white-eric-15809.

Here Come the Geisha Girls. (1959, August 3). *The Herald*, page unknown. In Black and White. (1959, September 11). *The Herald*, p. 3.

Knight, N. and Heazle, M. (2011). *Understanding Australia's Neighbours: An Introduction to East and Southeast Asia* (2nd edn). Port Melbourne, Australia: Cambridge University Press.

L'Etang, J. (2004). *Public Relations in Britain: A History of Professional Practice in the 20th Century*. Mahwah, NJ: Lawrence Erlbaum.

Oriental Cavalcade (1959, November 5). *Tharunka*, p. 4.

Rutledge, M. (2000). Martin, David Nathaniel (1898–1958). *Australian Dictionary of Biography*. Accessed 17 January 2020 from http://adb.anu.edu.au/biography/martin-david-nathaniel-11069/text19703.

Said, E. (1978). *Orientalism*. London, England: Routledge & Kegan Paul.

Sheehan, M. (2014). Australia. In T. Watson (Ed.) *Asian Perspectives on the Development of Public Relations: Other Voices* (pp. 4–13). Basingstoke, England: Palgrave.

She'll Get More Fans. (1959, August 4). *The Sun News-Pictorial*. p. 1.

Stewart, B. (2000). *A Survivor in a Star Spangled World*. East Blaxland, Australia: Author.

Tilson, D. J. (2017). Entertainment publicity and public relations. In T. Watson (Ed.), *North American Perspectives on the Development of Public Relations* (pp. 81–96). Basingstoke, England: Palgrave Macmillan.

Van Straten, F. (2003). *Tivoli*. South Melbourne, Australia: Lothian Books.

Walker, D. and Sobocinska, A. (Eds.) (2011). *Australia's Asia: From Yellow Peril to Asian Century*. Perth, Australia: UWA Publishing.

6 The militant documentary films of Helena Lumbreras as dissent and protest public relations

Isadora Guardia, Carolina Martínez and Jordi Xifra

Introduction

In recent years, the development of a critical perspective on public relations has highlighted the role of activism as one of the dimensions of public relations analysis (e.g., Brown, 2006; Holtzhausen, 2012; Demetrious, 2013; Heath & Xifra, 2016). In this framework, the concepts of *dissent public relations* and *protest public relations* (Moloney *et al.*, 2013) emerged; concepts that are similar to but different from public relations activism. Indeed,

> Dissent PR is ... about bringing attention to new thinking and new behaviours in areas of national life. It promotes ideas for change and for retention in the political economy and civil society. The term is not defined in a left-wing sense. Rather, it is PR promoting the ideas of public intellectuals, academics, experts and people of faith found in both progressive and conservative philosophical circles. It is PR techniques designed to bring attention to these thinkers and their arguments in order to change the policy climate. Dissent PR has a related form, Protest PR, which is a consequence of the 'dissent' term. It is also persuasive communication but not principally about ideas, behaviours and policies. Instead, it persuades in order to implement those ideas, behaviours and policies into law, regulation and other forms of executive action.
>
> (Moloney *et al.*, 2013: 3)

On the other hand but from the same approach, Brown (2006) argues that we have to rethink the concept of public relations as styles of perception and expression.

Among the most visible styles is activism, which continues to occupy the attention of issues management. Activism, which includes a variety of techniques, shares its uncompromising sensibility with that of the Faith Culture. The spectacle and performance techniques of activist public relations resonate with the sensibility of the Art Culture (Brown, 2006: 210).

This statement suggests the crucial role of performance techniques and media, such as film-making, in communicating activist and dissent positions. We often watch films as a means of analysing reality. The modes of representation of fiction films are of indisputable importance, offering an interpretation of the world that reflects our own image back at us, even proposing new ones (Imbert, 2010).

In the case of political or militant documentaries, the view of human existence is clearly much more complex. Reality is conceived as a referent and as a place where a dialogue can be established that allows the importance of representation, as a process inherent in cinematic construction, to be pushed into the background.

The intervention documentary deals with ongoing processes, understood as practices. The purpose of the study outlined in this article was to analyse and interpret a gendered and class-based political view of reality in Spain during a period of transition.

Helena Lumbreras' film-making practice offers us a construction of history *with and against* cinema[1] in a moment when the material conditions of production entailed a working approach that was largely clandestine.

Helena Lumbreras engages with the collective: the street, the factory, the class struggle and, within it, the restricted space of the working woman. This type of film-making is cinema against amnesia, according to Cerdán and Díaz López (2001: 13). In the case of Helena Lumbreras, this has been effectively reduced to the traces tracked by these two researchers on the relationships between the political, militant, gendered documentary and the reality of an era.

Delimitation of an era

Between 1967 and 1981,[2] a series of events took place in Spain that directly affected the relationship between cinema and reality, which constituted a period when the militant documentary film was at its peak. The Sitges Festival (1967) marked the beginning of a period of profound reflection on and reaction against what had been happening to cinema under the repressive Francoist regime. Meanwhile, with the failed coup d'état in 1981, a period of uncertainty in which revolutionary hopes ended. These two moments mark the rise and fall of a movement of hopeful, combative and militant cinema.

It is possible to identify film-making practices that battled not only to maintain a permanent space but also to raise a dissident voice against the dictatorship. The battle extended to a critique of the capitalist modes of production and a questioning of cinema as an 'ideological state apparatus' where the director is responsible for ensuring the replication of production relations.[3]

The increased availability of lighter cameras also facilitated the new film-making theories and practices that had already begun with the New American Cinema in the United States and the *Nouvelle Vague* in France, opening up the cinematic approach to reality not only in Spain but also all over the world (Ellis & McLane, 2005: 208). Militant films were screened at film clubs,[4] union halls, local churches and even factories (Linares, 1976: 32).[5]

In search of a term

The film-maker and theorist, Llorenç Soler, identifies the origins of the independent film-making movement in Spain as a circle in the 1950s that operated under the name of 'amateur cinema'. This 'amateur cinema' shares the concept with the one proposed by the avant-garde film-maker, Maya Deren (Ukraine 1917–United States 1961). She proposed the word '*amateur*' as a reaction against the spectacular, defending a cinema 'made with love' and without commercial purposes, making profit from the creative freedom offered by being marginal and working with limited technical means (Martínez, 2015). An offshoot of this group that turned towards social realism 'and away from a filmmaking practice with absolutely no artistic or cultural aspirations' (Romanguera & Soler, 2006: 19), which paved the way for an independent or alternative film movement that gradually began developing more politicised and interventionist approaches to the social reality.

The term 'militant' was adopted to refer to practices, which generally treated film-making as political action, as a tool or medium to challenge Francoism and capitalism; we can see this approach reflected in the films of Helena Lumbreras. Within this so-called militant movement, it was also possible to identify two distinct, although never really opposing, positions. On the one hand, some filmmakers advocated formal experimentation as a necessary means of combating the conventional mechanisms of communication and consumption; meanwhile, on the other hand, there were those who advocated the use of language that was accessible to spectators for whom their films were intended.[6]

Helena Lumbreras argued for a form of film-making that was not only political, industrial and social but also aesthetically revolutionary. She began her career in 1968 with *Spagna 68*, a clandestine film on the reality of the impact of May '68 in a Francoist Spain with a major social and political movement, which began long before any ray of hope could be glimpsed through the dark clouds of the dictatorship. It constitutes the most complete exploration of different grassroots organisations that were mobilising against Francoism in Spain.

Colectivo de Cine de Clase

The film-making collective known as Colectivo de Cine de Clase, formed by Helena Lumbreras and Mariano Lisa, was notable for its ideological consistency and its profound reflection on form. Helena Lumbreras was making this kind of work in the period from 1968 to 1978, first on her own and then in the collective (1973) with Mariano Lisa.[7]

Lumbreras, a teacher by training and profession, travelled to Italy and studied at the Centro Sperimentale di Cinematografia in Rome where she developed a strong political awareness, due in part to the influence of film-makers like Pier Paolo Pasolini.

At this time, Godard was distancing himself from the French New Wave to pursue a more politically active direction with the Dziga Vertov Group.

Meanwhile, in Latin America and especially in Argentina, there was a whole film-making movement reflected in examples like Getino and Solanas' *The Hour of the Furnaces* (La hora de los hornos, 1968), which would subsequently be distributed in Spain by collectives like La Central del Curt.

Lumbreras' films are notable for their militant and critical quality. Her film-making was controversial because it involved a commitment above and beyond the directives of the political parties. According to Mariano Lisa,[8] this commitment resulted in numerous problems for the documentary maker, as at times her stance went further than the official line of leftist organisations.

Lisa suggests that Helena Lumbreras was never comfortable in either the world of political activism or of film-making. Her dual status as woman and film-maker made for a certain uneasiness within this movement because, according to Lisa, chauvinism was rife among the Left. Moreover, in the context of a film world marked by a lack of experimentation and reflection, Lumbreras emerged as a film-maker[9] who went further than compiling direct testimony to develop political and cinematic discourses.

As Andrés Linares suggests, while other collectives were making a kind of express cinema, Colectivo de Cine de Clase was producing medium-length films on 16 mm with a recurring theme, which aimed to offer analysis and reflection on the situation of both the urban and rural working class, with a clear didactic and expository intention.[10]

Lumbreras understood that language had to be *re-adapted* according to the specific needs of each discourse, which always had to depend on their protagonists; in this case, the working class.

Lumbreras and Lisa suffered what was known among militants in Spain as a '*doble caída*' (double fall); arrested for their involvement in a strike, they were both dismissed from their jobs and expelled from the Communist Party of Spain.[11] They then went on to film *El Campo para el Hombre* [The Field for Men] (1973). This film marked the beginning of the collective's real work, focusing on the working-class struggle during the Francoist era and the subsequent transition to democracy.

In 1976, they made their second film, *O Todos o Ninguno* [All or None], about a labour dispute at a Catalan factory (Laforsa). It included footage filmed by the workers themselves, and the whole filming process was governed by consensus (Figure 6.1). On this question, important for its relevance to the objective of the interventionist documentary, the director herself debated with other film-makers and critics, including Manuel Esteban, Jesús Garay, Jaime Larrain, Joan Puig, Llorenç Soler, Pere Joan Ventura, Gustau Hernández and Ernest Blasi, in a round table discussion published by the magazine *El Viejo Topo* in 1977. In relation to the question of the use of cinematic language and whether the protagonists should be taught to make their own films, Helena Lumbreras argued:

> If we are trying to construct a discourse of class, of a class that will be the hegemonic class, that has a different world view, that discourse must necessarily be different from the discourse of the bourgeoisie. What the workers

Films as dissent and protest public relations 71

Figure 6.1 Still of *O todos o ninguno* (Colectivo de Cine de Clase, 1976) with Mariano Lisa, a worker and Helena Lumbreras. © LSP.

Figure 6.2 Still of *A la vuelta del grito* (Colectivo de Cine de Clase, 1977) showing the workers and their families closed in a church. © LSP.

at Laforsa filmed inside their factory is completely different from what [the national public broadcaster] TVE would have done, for example.[12]

Lumbreras' proposition thus represented an apparent qualitative leap from being the object to being the subject of the film, examining the very essence of the worker; at the same time, there may have been a potentially paternalistic view that would have undermined the conjunction of both historical and cinematic subject. In her own words, this meant that '[w]hen we try to give the working class some autonomy and promote their culture, we are doing something very dangerous'.

Colectivo de Cine de Clase continued to operate until 1977, when they made *A la Vuelta del Grito* [Back from the Scream], a film that had a more formal release (Figure 6.2). The film was not distributed by the collective itself since it dissolved immediately after making it, as did the vast majority of such collectives when the Transition began. In Lisa's words: 'It could be said that the Transition was a success on the political level but it obviously represented a veritable social disaster, accelerating the implementation in Spain of savage capitalism'.[13]

O Todos O Ninguno

O Todos o Ninguno (1976) deals with the worker struggle in the city. A 40-minute picture shot on 16 mm film in colour, it presents a labour dispute that led to a strike at a company called Laforsa in Cornellà (Barcelona), which lasted 106 days. This strike was notable as the longest in Catalonia since the end of the Civil War.

The documentary explores the rise of the worker movement during the death throes of Francoism, the presence of local movements and the solidarity with the rest of the working class which, in the period from Franco's death to the beginning of the 1980s, experienced an extraordinary degree of mobilisation (Ballester & Risques, 2001).

The film is dominated by a direct style, with the camera positioned close to the protagonists in the street and functioning as an amplifier for their voices. The main objective of this film is to dispute the ideological negation effectuated by conventional discourse when it attributes the workers' suffering to a private, emotional, supposedly authentic realm common to all human beings and therefore depicted as inevitable. However, in reality, it is due to processes shaped and organised by the prevailing economic system, which can be fought against (Adorno, 2013: 53).[14]

The illusory nature of this narrative is deliberately broken with the introduction to camera of the film-makers and protagonists. The place of the gaze is *from and to* the working class, and the blue overalls of the worker, like the statement to camera, render visible the production mechanisms and processes while focusing on the value of work (Zimmer, 1976: 52–54).[15]

This statement of intentions defines the film-making practice of the collective as a political, lived practice, turning the film-maker into a human being who makes films (García Merás, 2007: 16).[16]

The worker is introduced in the first person: 'I, Manuel González, dismissed in 1969 from Roca de Gavà, currently a worker at Laforsa…' Next to him, quite unusually, the members of the Collective as *us* in front of the camera *signing* the official statement.

The element that ties together and composes the structure is the journey that the workers make to bring their dispute to the rest of the town. It is a journey of importance that lies more in the encounter than in the journey's end (Bruzzi, 2006: 82).[17]

The workers' discussion in the school reflects the importance of teaching young people about a reality that is concealed in most cases, while getting them involved in the protest against it.

This is achieved through the creation of a mural painted by the boys and girls that tells the story of the conflict. This element also takes on a narrative value within the film, as illustrations, dates, activities, etc. that explain the development of the dispute and are inserted in a manner resembling inter-titles.

The action of taking the protest into the school becomes an exercise similar to that of taking cinema to the grassroots level, as proposed by Raymundo Gleyzer. The film thus constructs two levels of intervention; one is represented by the text and exists apart from it, which is the relationship between workers and students, while the other arises from the inclusion of this intervention in the film. The children listen and ask questions of the workers, who are also their parents, their role models. The frame of a children's drawing amplifies the violence of the event. The aim is to take the conflict to different core groups, including children, students, women, neighbourhoods, and other factories and companies, with the intention to explore how an apparently specific or individual situation, such as the dismissal of a few workers, has repercussions on the lives of a whole town.

The next sequence features the voice of the women. They are located initially at a table inside a house, in a space conventionally assigned to females. However, the action that takes place subverts the conventional appearance of the scene, as the women are writing an opinion letter to the newspaper explaining the repression that both they and their husbands are suffering. They verbalise the events of a few days earlier, such as the locking up of the workers in the church and the women's entry into the factory, in an attempt to occupy their husbands' work posts.[18] This time, the mode of representation is more reminiscent of a re-enactment.

This meeting to write an opinion letter actually occurred, although it happened before the film-makers could film it. At a meeting held by the collective with the workers and their wives, all agreed on the importance of this event and the need for the women to be present in the film because that was what was happening in reality. They therefore decided to re-enact the women's discussion, as well as their march through the streets dressed in worker overalls.

What is truly revealing in this sequence, as proof of the reality bursting forcefully into the cinematic space, is the everyday quality of life. In the fragment where the women discuss what to write, one of them explains while her small child interjects over the monologue to demand her attention.

The fact that an unintelligible child's voice should undermine a scripted narration in which the woman is explaining how the police entered the factory to evict them emphasises the pernicious nature of the enforcement officers' acts even more while also eliminating any hint of staging. The extraordinary alternates with the ordinary, blurring into reality and thereby demonstrating its existence, not as a subjective perception but as an autonomous fact (Bunge, 2007: 55).[19]

The inclusion of women's voices in the films of the collective is a constant; however, it clashes with an androcentric tradition that tacitly attributes the authority to develop discourse to the male voice. Lisa speaks of the need to make visible a sector of society that contributed just as much to the fight against Francoism, supporting freedom and social justice but undervalued within the leftist movement, as represented by the case of Helena Lumbreras herself, a concealed and silenced film-maker (Rodríguez Tejada, 2004: 123–146).

The film uses music in the final public act, addressed to the people of Cornellà, to signal that the general conflict is ongoing. In this way, importance is given to the historical/cinematic event, but without allowing its aesthetic value to undermine the quest for reality. The journey goes on, and this is expressed in the folk song in *O Todos o Ninguno*: '... *Esta copla no se acaba, que se ha de continuar, hasta el día que nuestra clase tenga victoria final*'. ['This copla never ends; it must go on until the day that our class has its final victory'.]

Thus, without abandoning its political stance, the persuasive implications of the story are limited by a deliberate rejection of the formal coherence of a complete, self-sufficient discourse. In this way, the documentary abandons the moral drama that characterises fiction (White, 1992) in favour of a kind of open ending typical of a report on a real historical process.

A La Vuelta del Grito

This 45-minute film marked the end of the film-making activity of Colectivo de Cine de Clase. Filmed in 1976 and 1977, it documents the worker mobilisations and political activity coordinated by the organisation Coordinadora de Empresas en Crisis, a coalition of different companies in Catalonia during this period. However, its focus is not limited to this region but also turns south to Andalusia and west to the industrial heartland of the Basque Country to construct a unified vision of the different spaces and to convey a sense of the universality of their struggle. This was a period of widespread mobilisations of workers and unions, including major strikes in Asturias (Köhler, 1995).

Although no specific reference is made in the film to specific events occurring simultaneously in that historical moment, such events form part of a country's collective consciousness or memory and serve as a *trigger* for that memory, facilitating a better understanding of the message in the text.

Adopting a genuinely Marxist perspective, the objective proposed in the documentary is the rejection of ideology as a necessary illusion through a critique of reality that exposes the truth that the events and their interpretation, while apparently neutral, are in fact the specific result of the confrontation between political and social forces (Lenk, 2002: 25). To this end, the film is constructed using the following elements:

Inter-titles have a didactic function to explicate the process of the economic crisis afflicting the country at the time and to link it to a broader international crisis: 'The capitalist system periodically experiences so-called crises of overexploitation'.

Real testimonies and images have the function of documenting and demonstrating the material consequences of the situation described in the inter-titles.

The organisation of these elements articulates the structure of the film. The official narrative is replaced with a presentation of events that acquire their real meaning in the editing process, an element of special importance in this documentary because of the cognitive dissonance it creates. The still shot of a watchful leopard that opens the film lasts for more than twenty seconds.

Above the illustration, a quote by the Trotskyist theorist Ernest Mandel[20] reads: 'The leopard has not changed its spots; capitalism is always capitalism: its internal contradictions remain unsolvable'.[21]

This cuts to a sequence shot filmed with a hand-held camera, panning around a church hall where some men are laying down mattresses and resting while women with children in their arms look on.

Once again the presence of the woman appears as a voice projected from two spaces. On the one hand, she is included in the film's social voice in the inter-titles that represent the woman sewing as an 'exploited worker'; on the other hand, the women's participation in each protest action is portrayed. In this way, the women occupy a place and a gaze throughout the film due to their visibility, and their capacity to develop a gendered discourse distanced from the standardising voice referred to by Bruzzi (2006). Women are represented as part of the working class, breaking out of private spaces to enter into the contexts of the struggle, as well as being asserted with the dual status of gender and class. Thus, the construction of a gendered discourse, in which women's dual status is explained as an element of a dual struggle, exposes the voice that remains concealed under the more orthodox tradition of the worker movement.

In the sequence showing the Eurostil dispute, the women initiate a debate on the influence of certain unions and their interference in the decisions of the female workers, where some feel restricted by the workers' committee itself (Rodríguez Tejada, 1995). This capacity to develop a critical discourse is acknowledged by Lisa when he explains the shooting process.[22]

In this way, the street and, in some cases, private spaces like the home become public spaces for debate and action (Babiano, 2007). It is precisely in such spaces that the woman's presence acquires visibility to contrast with no image in more conventional depictions of such struggles. It is not a female gaze on reality but a class-based gaze that views the presence of the woman's voice in historical processes as a real and indispensable fact.

Conclusions

Helena Lumbreras' filmography sheds light on the dual task of women in the private, domestic sphere when that sphere is turned into a space for struggle and intervention while they also seek to maintain their place in the working world. From this perspective, Helena Lumbreras' films have the same purposes of the first documentary makers, such as Grierson, Ivens, Malraux, Buñuel and others. Indeed, she used documentaries for social change, she went further and made a type of film in which the authorship was endorsed to those who were spokespersons for advocacy messages. Her purpose was to use the camera as a real weapon of dissent and protest, for capturing the truth and playing a real role of activist public relations, that is, the defence of a counter-hegemonic position with regard to the conventional production system.

To sum up, Helena Lumbreras was a big (and forgotten) name of Spanish dissent and protest PR because she uses documentaries to achieve real social change in Spain. She was a deserving successor of other big (and forgotten names) of PR film practitioners because she followed Grierson's documentary principle: to use real people in their own environments with a persuasive purpose.

Notes

1 The phrase in italics here alludes to the text with the title *Con y contra el cine. En torno a Mayo del 68* [With and against Cinema: On May '68], which came out of the project *Mayo del 68: el comienzo de una época* [May '68: The Beginning of an Era], coordinated by Universidad Internacional de Andalucía (UNIA), Sociedad Estatal de Conmemoraciones Culturales and Fundació Antoni Tàpies in 2008.
2 We concur with the delimitation of the period established by Lydia García-Merás in her article 'El cine de la disidencia. La producción militante antifranquista (1967–1981)' in Jesús Carrillo et al. (Eds.) (2007). *Desacuerdos 4. Sobre arte, políticas y esfera pública en el Estado español,* Granada: Arteleku-MACBA-UNIA, pp. 16–38. On the other hand, Llorenç Soler and Joaquim Romanguera identify the existence of an independent film-making movement in Spain, which would encompass other definitions between the years 1955 and 1975, at which point the movement progressively dissolved. Cf. Joaquim Romaguera and Llorenç Soler (2006). *Historia crítica y documentada del cine independiente en España. 1955–1975,* Barcelona: Alertes.
3 Much of the debate in the militant film movement in this period arose from the adoption of the concept of ideology established by Althusser, whereby cinema was classified together with the school and the church as an ideological state apparatus. See Louis Althusser, 'Ideología y aparatos ideológicos del Estado' at www.infoamerica.org/documentos_pdf/althusser1.pdf.
4 '1956 was the year of the creation of what at the time was called the National Federation of Film Clubs …, a movement which in many cases would also participate in the dissemination of a non-professional film movement that was assertive, rebellious, avant-garde and innovative'. Romanguera and Soler, *Historia crítica y documentada,* p. 21.
5 Pere Joan Ventura recalls that on one occasion, a film of a demonstration in Barcelona was screened in an automobile repair shop. Interview with Pere Joan Ventura, Madrid, 22 November 2007.
6 This debate went on from the end of the 1960s and throughout the 1970s, in both France and Italy; it had also already begun in Argentina with two 'opposing' groups: Grupo Cine Liberación de Getino y Solanas and Cine de la Base de Gleyzer. The need to establish a language that would subvert the institutional modes of representation, even before they were perpetuated, was already identified by Dziga Vertov in the early 1920s.
7 See also the cases of Marie Menken and Willard Maaas, Mary Ellen Bute and Theodor Nemeth, Maya Deren and Alexander Hammid, Carole Roussopoulos and Paul Roussopoulos (collectif Video Out), Delphine Seyrig and Sami Frey, or the Colombian Marta Rodríguez and her husband.

8 Interview with Mariano Lisa 3/2008.
9 As pointed by Rabinovitz (2003) regarding New York avant-garde women filmmakers, the marginalised position of women in cinema had the advantage of offering them greater expressive freedom. For this reason, the most radical works in certain cinematographic movements have come very often from the hands of women (most of them writing also their own film theory), although, in many cases, they have remained invisible.
10 Linares, interview cited above.
11 Mariano Lisa explains that their arrest caused 'suspicion among their militant comrades, even though nobody else was involved. The chasm was so huge that in addition to expulsion from the party, many friends changed their addresses and even refused to talk to them'. Interview cited above.
12 Various Authors, 'Cine militante', pp. 47–59. The quotes included in the following paragraphs come from the same round table discussion published in the magazine.
13 Mariano Lisa took part in the round table 'Documentales: información y contrainformación', organised by Universidad Internacional de Andalucía, Seminar: *Medios de masas, multitud y prácticas antagonistas (Desacuerdos-UNIA)*, www2.unia.es/artpen/ezine/ezine01_2005/main.html.
14 'As it runs in the jargon: suffering, evil and death are to be accepted, not to be changed. The public is being trained in this tour de force of maintaining a balance. They are learning to understand their Nothingness as being, to revere actual, avoidable or, at least, corrigible need as the most humane element in the image of Man. They are learning to respect authority in itself because of their innate human insufficiency'. Theodor W. Adorno, *The Jargon of Authenticity*, London: Routledge, 2013 (1964), p. 53.
15 With respect to the enunciation of the processes for meaning production in cinema from a Marxist perspective, it is necessary to break the bond between the narration and the ideologically based objective of spectacle to approach the precise, the rigorous and the profound. See Christian Zimmer, *Cine y política*, Salamanca: Sígueme, 1976, pp. 52–54.
16 As Helena Lumbreras expresses it: 'We are not making film history; we are making history with film'.
17 This type of journey, differentiated from the 'road movie' by the greater importance it gives to what happens along the way than to the conclusion, is defined by Bruzzi as a 'travelogue'. The film-makers and the audience discover what happens together with the protagonists.
18 This idea of women intervening and even taking on their husbands' jobs is depicted in what is considered the first militant film in history: *Salt of the Earth*, directed by Herbert Biberman in 1954.
19 'Real things are those that exist independently of any subject', states Bunge in his text on reality.
20 German economist and politician (Frankfurt, 1923-Brussels, 1995). www.ernestmandel.org/es.
21 This quote is an allusion to an Old Testament verse: 'Can an Ethiopian change his skin or a leopard its spots? Neither can you do good who are accustomed to doing evil'. Jeremiah 13: 23.
22 Lisa explains how the women had no qualms about debating in front of the camera while, in the case of the men, their 'activism' prompted them to be less explicit, even though they did hold the same view as the women. Mariano Lisa, interview 15 March 2008, Barcelona.

References

Adorno, Theodor W. (2013 [1964]). *The Jargon of Authenticity*, London: Routledge.
Augé, M. (2001). *Los no lugares. Espacios del anonimato. Una antropología de la sobremodernidad*, Barcelona: Gedisa.
Babiano, J. (ed.) (2007). *Del hogar a la huelga: estudios sobre trabajo, género y movimiento obrero bajo el franquismo*, Madrid: Los Libros de la Catarata.
Ballester, D. & Risques, M. (2001). *Temps d'amnistia. Les manifestacions de l'1 i el 8 de febrer a Barcelona*, Barcelona: Edicions 62.
Barnouw, E. (2005). *El documental. Historia y estilo*, Barcelona: Gedisa.
Blanco, L. (1996). La escuela oficial del cine. El Instituto de Investigaciones y Experiencias Cinematográficas. In Pedro Medina et al., *Historia del cortometraje español*, Alcalá de Henares: Festival de Cine de Alcalá de Henares-Comunidad de Madrid-Ayuntamiento de Alcalá de Henares-Filmoteca de la Generalitat Valenciana-Conselleria de Cultura de la Comunidad Valenciana.
Brown, R. (2006). Myth of symmetry public relations as cultural styles. In *Public Relations Review*, 32, 206–212.
Bruzzi, S. (2006). *New Documentary*, London: Routledge.
Bunge, M. (2007). *A la caza de la realidad. La controversia sobre el realismo*, Barcelona: Gedisa.
Carrillo, J. (ed.) (2007). *Desacuerdos 4. Sobre arte, políticas y esfera pública en el Estado español*, Granada: Arteleku-MACBA-UNIA
Cerdán, J. & y Díaz López, M. (2001). *Cecilia Bartolomé. El encanto de la lógica*, Madrid: Ocho y Medio.
Demetrious, K. (2013). *Public Relations, Activism, and Social Change: Speaking up*, New York: Routledge.
Ellis, Jack C. & McLane, Betsy A. (2005). *A New History of Documentary Film*, New York: Continuum.
García-Merás, L. (2007). El cine de la disidencia. La producción militante antifranquista (1967–1981). In Jesús Carrillo et al. (Eds.), *Desacuerdos 4. Sobre arte, políticas y esfera pública en el Estado español*, Granada: Arteleku-MACBA-UNIA.
Guardia, I. (2011). *El documental como herramienta de intervención social. El caso Sintel*, Berlin: EAE.
Gubern, R. et al. (1995). *Historia del cine español*, Madrid: Cátedra.
Hartt, F. (1989). *Arte. Historia de la pintura, escultura y arquitectura*, Madrid: Akal.
Heath, R. L. & Xifra, J. (2016). What is critical about critical public relations theory? In L'Etang, J., McKie, D., Snow, N. & Xifra, J. (Eds.), *The Routledge Handbook of Critical Public Relations* (pp. 200–210), New York: Routledge.
Holtzhausen, D. (2012). *Public Relations as Activism: Postmodern Approaches to Theory and Practice*, New York: Routledge.
Imbert. G. (2010). *Cine e imaginarios sociales*, Madrid: Cátedra.
Köhler, H.-D. (1995), El movimiento sindical en España. Transición democrática – modernización económica – region-alismo, Madrid: Ed. Fundamentos, 1995 (2ª ed. 2001).
Lenk, K. (2002). *El concepto de ideología. Comentario crítico y selección sistemática de documentos*, Buenos Aires: Amorrortu.
Linares, A. (1976). Cine y clandestinidad en España. In P. Medina et al., *Historia del cortometraje español*, Madrid: Festival de Alcalá de Henares.

Lozano, J. et al. (1989). *Análisis del discurso. Hacia una semiótica de la interacción textual*, Madrid: Cátedra.
Maqua, J. (1992). *El docudrama. Fronteras de la ficción*, Madrid: Cátedra.
Martínez, C. & Deren, M. (2015). *El universo dereniano. Textos fundamentales de la cineasta Maya Deren*, Cuenca: Publicaciones de la Universidad de Castilla-La Mancha y Artea Editorial.
Moloney, K., McQueen, D., Surowiec, P. & Yaxley, H. (2013). *Dissent and protest public relations*, Bournemouth: Public Relations Research Group, The Media School, Bournemouth University.
Mukarovsky, J. (1977). *Escritos de estética y semiótica del arte*, Barcelona: Gustavo Gili.
Nieto, J. & Company, J. M. (eds.) (2006). *Por un cine de lo real. Cincuenta años después de las "Conversaciones de Salamanca"*, Valencia: IVAC-Generalitat Valenciana.
Piault, M. H. (2002). *Antropología y cine*, Madrid: Cátedra.
Rabinovitz, L. (2003). *Points of Resistance. Women, Power & Politics in the New York Avant-garde Cinema, 1943–71*, Chicago: University of Illinois Press.
Rodríguez Tejada, S. (1995). La otra igualdad. Feminismo y discurso sindical sobre la mujer. In Pilar Calvo (ed.), *Discriminación de género en la negociación colectiva del País Valenciano*, Valencia: Generalitat Valenciana-Tirant Lo Blanch-CCOO.
Rodríguez Tejada, S. (2004). Compañeras: la militancia de las mujeres en el movimiento antifranquista en Valencia. *Historia del Presente*, 4, 123–146.
Romanguera, J. and Soler, ll. (2006) *Historia crítica y documentada del cine independiente en España 1955–1975*, Barcelona: Laertes.
Sánchez-Biosca, V. (2006). *Cine de historia, cine de memoria*. Madrid: Cátedra.
Vertov, D. (1984). From kino-eye to radio-eye. In Annette Michelson (ed.), *Kino-Eye: The Writings of Dziga Vertov*, Los Angeles: University of California Press.
VVAA (1977). El cine militante en revista *El Viejo Topo*, Barcelona.
White, H. (1992 [1987]). *El contenido de la forma. Narrativa, discurso y representación histórica*, Barcelona: Paidós.
White, H. (1992 [1973]). *Metahistoria. La imaginación histórica en la Europa del siglo XIX*, México City: FCE.
Zimmer, C. (1976). *Cine y política*, Salamanca: Sígueme.

7 A 'herstory' of Malaysian public relations
Paddy Schubert, Malaysia's women PR pioneer

Rizwanah Souket

Introduction

The role of women is often neglected or in the background or most often absorbed within male hegemony in an anxious attempt to assert the professional status of the public relations discipline through written histories and biographies. Several scholars have highlighted this discrepancy and argue that women's historical contributions to public relations are often marginalized (L'Etang, 2015; Fitch, 2016). Malaysia is no different when it comes to neglecting women in the written histories of Malaysian public relations. Souket and Idid (2020) state that the first traces of Malaysian public relations began with the formation of an organized information agency in 1910. Later, the Department of Information of 1939 and the Department of Information and Publicity of 1940 paved the way for the first Department of Public Relations in Malaysia in 1946. In these written records, the documented forerunners of Malaysian public relations were often the first directors of the information departments. Souket (2019) traced the history of public relations in Malaysia, recording the contributions of Sir William Taylor, a retired Resident General, in setting up the 1910 Information Agency; G.L. Peet, a veteran journalist with *Straits Times*, as Director of the Department of Information of 1939; Victor Purcell, a civil servant and a counter-intelligence officer, as Director of the Department of Information and Publicity of 1940 and M. C. Sheppard, a Malayan civil service officer, as the first Director of the Department of Public Relations in 1946. However, the role of women in the history of Malaysian public relations has been significantly neglected; in fact, there is no record of a woman's contribution to the development of public relations in Malaysia. This chapter is the first scholarly attempt in documenting a herstory of one woman's successes and contributions to Malaysian public relations. Paddy Schubert (now called Paddy Bowie), a British-born Malaysian public relations pioneer, has contributed immensely to Malaysian public relations. She is a prolific writer, activist, practitioner, leader, counsel and pioneer educationist. This chapter documents a herstory of Paddy Schubert and her 60 years' experience in Malaysian public relations.

The early years: Pearl Margaret Mary Fort of Lancashire

Paddy Schubert was born on 11 May 1925 and was christened as Pearl Margaret Mary Fort at St Leonard's Church in Padiham in Lancashire, England. Schubert decided to call herself Paddy when she was leaving home for the first time, at the age of 20, to pursue her studies. The name 'Paddy' was used to allude her hometown (Padiham), and the name has remained with her (Schubert, 2018).

As an only child, Paddy had a very outgoing and gregarious personality, which was one of her greatest assets in later life. Her close friend, Malcolm Williams, describes her in an interview: 'company stimulates her, I don't think she will ever retire, not in the real sense of the word' (Ruhanie, 2007). Today, Paddy, at the age of 95, has the ability to put people at ease (Bowie, 2020, personal interview, 31 January). In her personal memoir, Paddy describes herself as an extrovert child eager to explore and make friends (Schubert, 2018). At a very early age, Paddy had a knack for adventures and has written on how she used to love exploring the mysterious Pendle Hill in her home town which was then a very isolated hill famous for wolves, wild boars and as a legendary home of witches and warlocks. She aspired to be a journalist or a lawyer, but those occupations were reserved for men, while women were restricted to nursing, secretarial or teaching. Paddy chose to take up teaching and later describes the teaching profession as 'the nurturing profession extending women's traditional role of looking after the men' (Schubert, 2018: 10). Subsequently, Paddy's studies were interrupted with World War II, and she had to work in a factory when, during this period, she confronted the horrors of the war. Soon after the war was over, Paddy decided to pursue her studies and gained admission into Manchester University to enrol for a diploma in education. Later, she attended St. Anne's College in Oxford for postgraduate work where she became acquainted with people like Margaret Thatcher, future British Conservative Prime Minister, and Tony Benn, a leading left-wing Labour politician. Her passion to explore and experience adventure led her to apply for teaching positions overseas. Schubert was offered a position teaching English in Singapore and left in 1955 for the tiny British colony in British Malaya with five other English girls. She recorded her feelings in her personal memoir:

> I was a veritable Daughter of Empire but a perverse one. I was meant to grow up and marry the boy next door. Instead, I found myself as a young, inexperienced teacher bound for one of our distant outposts. I didn't know what to expect, back in 1955.
>
> (Schubert, 2018: 11)

Hence, she began her journey to Malaya.

Paddy Schubert: *en route* to Malaysian public relations

Following World War II, British Malaya was in a state of chaos and unrest, marked by riots and demonstrations all over Malaya (Ryan, 1965). On 1 February 1948, the Federation of Malaya was established in an attempt to unify British control over the Malayan territories. As a result, the British were increasingly detested by the Malays who had lost faith in British Governance and felt the British had betrayed their interests with the formation of the Federation. A state of emergency was declared by the British government in an attempt to control the guerrilla insurgency prompted by the Communist party of Malaya (Ryan, 1965). The Malayan Emergency ran from 16 June 1948 to 31 July 1960. It was during these precarious moments in Malaya that Paddy Schubert made her entrance as a teacher in Singapore, British Malaya.

Paddy records her first experience of meeting the Malayan people in her memoir. 'The people were friendly but greeted you not with "How do you do: How are you?" but the universal "have you eaten?"', a tell-tale sign of the poverty and deprivations faced by their ancestors many generations before (Schubert, 2018: 14). Paddy's unorthodox appeal (though being an English woman) eased her ability to mingle with the local community. She describes in her memoir how she used to enjoy eating the local cuisine with her fingers. Paddy has mentioned on several occasions her disapproval of English customs that were often very male dominated. She speaks of how social life in Singapore was 'not quite apartheid but strictly segregated' (Schubert, 2018: 15) and how the clubs were only meant for the colonial masters who have to be dressed with black tie and formal attire despite the heat of Malaya.

Paddy was appointed in 1955 to teach communication and skills of advocacy at a Law department for a local tertiary institution that was later to become the National University of Singapore (NUS). She was appointed for a period of five years, and many of Paddy's students are now prominent personalities in the Malaysian law and political community. Paddy records her students fondly in her memoir: 'Tommy Koh and Jayakumar were among my first batches of students. If I ever commit murder, I'll have stout alumni both sides of the Causeway to defend me and half the judges will have to rescue themselves' (Schubert, 2018: 16).

It was also during this time, as a statement of her unorthodox charisma, she breached the white standard customs and broke the colour bar in 1958 by marrying a local. Her first husband was Matthew Carl Schubert (known as Carl), a local of Ceylonese origin. He had joined Raffles College in Singapore in 1940 and was a staunch cricket player, as well as being an advocate and solicitor for the city council. Carl Schubert was later appointed President of the Singapore Cricket Association in 1962. When Paddy married Carl, she went against the local British society and crossed the existing racial barrier and social divide, triggering disapproval from the British community in Singapore. 'I was upset but very much in love. Exile, however, was the best thing that happened to me. It plunged me into the local scene' (Schubert, 2018: 21). In 1960, Paddy was recruited as a training officer to conduct English classes for executives and managers at Shell Singapore. She continued for three years until she decided to move to Kuala Lumpur in 1963.

Meanwhile in British Malaya, on 31 August 1957, Tunku Abdul Rahman took the oath of office as the first Prime Minister of an independent Malaya. In 1963, the Federation of Malaysia was formed when Sabah, Singapore and Sarawak joined the Federation of Malaya agreement. In August 1965, Malaysia's parliament voted to expel Singapore from the Federation.

Paddy had the opportunity to experience the birth and growth of a new nation – Malaysia: 'the Siamese twins, Singapore and Malaysia, joined at the hip (the causeway) and inextricably linked by race, culture, history and tradition, were separated by political surgery' (Schubert, 2018: 28). After the separation of Singapore from the Federation, Paddy decided to stay in Malaysia. She recalls her decision in her memoir: 'Malaysia was different. Confronted with such diverse population, they chose integration not assimilation … In a fast globalizing and interconnecting world, little Malaysia finds itself a role model of multi-racial and inter-cultural management' (Schubert, 2018: 29). She was granted citizenship by the Malaysian Prime Minister, Tunku Abdul Rahman, in 1963 and has since lived in Malaysia. 'I like the people here and how diverse they are. I like the fact that they practice integration by keeping their languages, cultures and traditions' (Schubert, 2018: 32).

The year 1960 was very important for Paddy as it was the year when she adopted her first son, a Chinese boy, in Singapore on 28 December 1960. She named him Peter Schubert. It was also in this year that Paddy began her career in the oil industry by joining Shell Singapore as a training officer. Two years later, in 1962, Paddy adopted her second son, Richard Schubert. When Paddy moved to Kuala Lumpur in 1963, it was the Malayan Emergency period, and she had witnessed the British warfare measures taken to curb the uprising of communist power. She records descriptions of the villages set up for the Chinese and how she was searched for carrying firearms or food supplies when travelling up-country. In Malaysia, Paddy adopted her third child, a daughter whom she called Samantha Schubert. 'My personal gain from the 1969 riots was the gift of a daughter. She was an abandoned baby of Kiwi-Sino parentage in the Assunta hospital' (Schubert, 2018: 36). Samantha is renowned in Malaysia as Miss Malaysia-World 1991 and later as a successful actress and producer (*The Star*, 2016). Paddy always spoke of the importance of family and children. In her memoir, she records her children's school life and outings. On one occasion when attending an International Conference, Paddy voiced that children should never be neglected, and a career woman should schedule her time for her children (*The Straits Times*, 1977a: 15).

Tragedy hit Paddy's family in 1975 when Carl Schubert died of a stroke in the KL General Hospital, leaving Paddy a widow with three children. After five years, she married a Briton, John Bowie, a marketing controller at the Malaysian Mining Corporation, and took the name Paddy Bowie. Heartbreak struck again when John Bowie died of liver complications on 14 March 1998. To add to the series of tragedies in Paddy's life, she lost her son Peter in 2004 to a car accident and, two years later, her second son, Richard, died of an illness. In 2016, she lost her daughter Samantha to cancer. The despair and heartbreak of losing her family members devastated her, and she took a long time to recover.

Paddy Schubert: reaching the helm of success in Malaysian public relations

At a time when women in public relations were largely invisible, Paddy Schubert successfully fought male hegemony and opened the doors for several Malaysian women to find success. The strength of public relations in a country depends on the quality of education and training provided. Paddy has fulfilled this need as a pioneer educationist and being the first Malaysian public relations course director.

After leaving Singapore, Paddy took up a teaching job at a local college, MARA College in Malaysia. MARA College began its operations in November 1957 as RIDA (Rural & Industrial Development Authority) Training Centre, which focused on helping rural Malays. Today, the college is a public university known as Mara University of Technology. Soon after, Paddy was recruited back to Shell Malaysia as a Shell Co. training officer and gradually worked her way up to attain Board Member status. The Shell Transport and Trading Company has had a presence in Malaysia since they first struck oil in Miri Sarawak in 1910. Since then, Shell has grown exponentially as one of the leading petroleum retail markets in Malaysia. In 1969, after moving through various posts in personnel and public relations, Schubert was appointed as the Trade Relations Manager of the Shell companies in Malaysia and Singapore, responsible for Shell's public relations (*The Straits Times*, 1969). Soon after, Paddy was appointed to the main board of the Shell Group of companies in Malaysia and Singapore, thus making her the first woman in the worldwide Shell Group to attain Board Member status. She was later promoted as the Group Director of Shell companies in Malaysia and Singapore. Paddy's thoughts on her experience working in a male-dominated industry:

> During my twenty years of corporate experience in Shell, I was the only woman amongst all those macho reservoir engineers and what had been a male chauvinist preserve. But in the end, there was no gender bias. Malaysia stood out in the international Shell world as the first to appoint a woman director to the main board of an operating company.
>
> (Schubert, 2018: 51)

Her greatest contribution to Malaysian public relations was to become a council member of the Institute of Public relations in Malaysia (IPRM). IPRM was formed in 1962 with the sole purpose of benefitting the public relations fraternity in Malaysia (Idid, 2005). To enhance the standard of public relations in Malaysia, IPRM council members decided to conduct formal education and training programmes. This was a first step taken in Malaysia to qualify the status of the public relations practitioners and to enhance the industry's reputation (Idid, 2005). Two members, L. M. Anderson and Peter Clague, were appointed course directors and charged with proposing the introductory course in public relations. However, one of the directors, Anderson, left for Australia and IPRM therefore had to find a 'heavyweight PR personality' (Morais 2020, personal communication, 18 April) to steer the course, which was where Paddy Schubert came in.

Paddy was appointed as the course director, thus making her the First Malaysian PR educator. An education and training committee was formed under her to run the academic programme. On 9 March 1971, IPRM began the first introductory course in public relations. Syed Arabi Idid, a former IPRM president (1993–1997), recorded the details of the academic programme in his book *Institute of Public Relations Malaysia: A Historical Perspective* (Idid, 2005). The first course run by Paddy welcomed enrolment of 74 Malaysians, ran twice weekly for four months and was conducted in the posh Shell Malaysia's training auditorium. Idid (2005) records that only 45 of the 74 Malaysians who had enrolled for the course passed the examinations. Out of the successful 45, 17 were women, with three of the top four scoring distinctions. For Paddy, the successful results implied that 'the public relations fraternity in Malaysia is by no means an exclusive preserve of the males' (Idid, 2005: 72). As the course director, Paddy was responsible for scheduling and monitoring the progress of the course, identifying relevant lecturers, preparing examination questions, supervising the grading and releasing marks to the students. The lecturers were selected from amongst the members, practitioners and academics, being paid a minimal sum and supporting the programme mainly as volunteers (Idid, 2005), thus often leaving the course director to face the difficulties of dealing with absent lecturers. Paddy Schubert, along with G. Bradshaw and Lye Peng Chan, were appointed as members of the Board of Examiners to oversee matters related to examinations for the introductory course. The first batch of Schubert's students received their certificates from the Minister for Special Functions and Information. Five years later, with the success of the introductory programme, the IPRM introduced the next level, the Intermediate Public Relations Programme, in 1976. The IPRM continued to run these courses for a number of years before, in 1982, introducing its first Diploma Course in Public Relations in collaboration with the Communication, Advertising and Marketing (CAM) Education Foundation, London.

Under Paddy's direction, the courses attracted many participants from the private sector as well as participants from government departments, such as Tenanga Nasional, Telekom Malaysia, ASPs, DSPs and Superintendents from the Police, and officers from the Army, Navy and Air Force (Morais 2020, personal communication, 18 April). Benedict V. Morais, her former student and later President of IPRM from 1987 to 1989, shares his experience with Paddy:

> She taught corporate communications, crisis communications and even led us in case study discussions. She also regularly supported IPRM's efforts by placing adverts in our publications, especially our quarterly journal. She was also readily available to take part in IPRM colloquiums, conferences or seminars. This lent considerable prestige to our events by such high-level participation.
>
> (Morais 2020, personal communication, 18 April)

Paddy was the first woman to be elected into the IPRM council and the first woman to serve as Vice President of IPRM from 1976 to 1978. She was elected as an honorary member of IPRM on 27 March 1983. Soon after the 17th Council member meeting in 1979, Paddy became less active and gradually left IPRM. However, even after she left, she supported IPRM's efforts. On one occasion, she collaborated with IPRM members and wrote a chapter (International Relations) for a special IPRM publication, World Class Public Relations in Practice, dedicated to Dr. Mahathir Mohamad. On another occasion, IPRM organized an international event called the Great Debate and brought teams from two renowned universities, Oxford University and Cambridge University. The debate was held on 2 April 1988, and more than 900 people attended. Paddy participated as a speaker for the Oxford team, while Dr. Goh Cheng Trik, a former deputy minister, spoke for the Cambridge team.

Below is an excerpt from a letter dated 6 April 1988 sent by Paddy to Benedict Morais. Benedict Morais was then president of IPRM:

> I must congratulate the Institute on what I consider the single most successful venture undertaken by the institute in all the years I have been associated with it. We are an ideas profession and this was a winner. What is more appropriate than for a professional association whose trade mark is communications to organize a contest of oratory? As hardened professionals, we know that it would not have seized the media's attention the way it did had it not had news value for breaking new ground.
>
> (Morais 2020, personal communication, 18 April)

Paddy was also affiliated with another professional organization, the Malaysian Institute of Management (MIM), which was formed in 1966 to introduce the art and practice of management skills to Malaysians (Malaysian Institute of Management, 2018). Paddy was a founder member of the Governing Council of MIM and remained its chairman for many years. She was awarded the honour of being appointed to the Court of Emeritus Fellows of MIM, thus making her the first woman in the organization to be elected to the inaugural governing council and appointed as the first woman chairman. Later, she served as President of the regional body, the Asia Association of Management Organizations (AAMO), thus being the first woman to take up the position and the first Malaysian to Chair the Association. During her involvement, she had addressed several world management congresses in Munich, Caracas, New Delhi, Lima, Adelaide and Kuala Lumpur (Schubert, 2018).

After 20 years of serving Shell, Paddy decided to start her own strategic communications company with her close friend Mary McEvoy. In 1980, Paddy founded the Paddy Schubert Consultants Sdn Bhd.

> Later on, I cast off the constraints and the comfort of the Shell cocoon to continue the journey of self-development. I chose to practice public relations and found I had one distinct advantage. Most of my fellow practitioners were

highly proficient in the professional skills required but had no real exposure to business at the operating level. PR is recognized now as an integral part of the Business Plan but Board level and corporate experience is a rare asset. We would be there involved in the policy and decision-making level when the bricks are being made, not just called in to pick up the bricks when they fall apart.

(Schubert, 2018: 53)

It was after the set-up of her own PR consultancy that Schubert ventured into a broad spectrum of businesses, political analysis and consultancy services. As a political consultant, she has contributed to news articles and worked behind the scenes as a speech writer for a few well-known cabinet ministers at that time. Below is an excerpt from an article during the 1999 election period, when the then prime minister, Tun Mahathir, was facing a political crisis in the country.

'The Malaysia-bashing by the foreign media has precipitated a crisis of confidence focused on Dr. Mahathir', says Paddy Schubert, a political-risk consultant in Kuala Lumpur. 'He's anathema to them because he's been painted as a despot'. But she adds: 'Once he wins a democratic election, they will re-evaluate their options'.

(Jayasankaran, 1999)

Paddy is a prolific writer, and some of the famous books she wrote as a PR consultant include *Vision Realised* (Story of Petronas), *The Entrepreneur Banker* (on Azman Hashim). As a political and business analyst, she has written and contributed to several publications, such as *Fortune* magazine, the *Economist*, *News Straits Times*, British Malaysian Chamber of Commerce, *Expat* and *Homme* magazines, *Washington Post*, etc., on topics related to government relations, issues management, corporate affairs and investment advice. She has written and produced many documentaries and films, such as the award-winning film on Sarawak entitled *Where the Rivers Meet*. Her documentaries mainly focused on the oil industry and included *Flame from the Forest*. Paddy was also commissioned to work on a film about Dr. Mahathir that included video interviews with 30 global leaders, including Margaret Thatcher, Henry Kissinger, Nelson Mandela, Bill Gates and others (Schubert, 2018).

Paddy was active in providing skills training, very much related to her first job in Shell. Her workshops included media training interview techniques, negotiation skills, public speaking, spokesperson training, crisis management and induction programmes for expatriates where she briefed prospective investors on the political culture of Malaysia and investment opportunities. These workshops were well received and attracted many political and corporate leaders. During an interview conducted on 31 January 2020, Anil Pillay, the Executive Director of Paddy Schubert Consultants and Paddy's adviser since 2009, recounts: 'her communications skills were the best I have ever seen, even to this day. She had a way of making things, and persons come alive when she was re-telling her stories

... I always remember her words: "Each speech is a performance, and should be treated as such"'.

To add to her accomplishments, Paddy won several notable awards, both locally and internationally. In 2007, she was awarded the Order of the British Empire (OBE) in recognition of her invaluable contributions to the United Kingdom and Malaysia. In 2011, she was awarded the most Honourable Order of the Crown of Perak – Knight Commander, the Darjah Dato' Panduka Mahkota Perak (DPMP), which gave her the title of Datuk, in recognition of her invaluable contributions to Malaysia.

Paddy Schubert: championing women at work

Paddy broke the glass ceiling many years ago when she became the first woman to attain Board Member status in the worldwide Shell Group. Since then, her accomplishments, as the first woman elected into the IPRM council, the first woman Chairman of the MIM council, first woman to Chair the regional AAMO and as a pioneer in PR education, have greatly impacted career advancements and opportunities for Malaysian women. Shahreen Kamaluddin, a Senior Fellow of IPRM and a former PR manager who had worked under Paddy, recalls Paddy as a '*true blue blood* PR professional' who brought stature to PR practice in the Shell Group of companies (Kamaluddin 2020, personal interview, 20 April).

Paddy became a visible advocate for the recruitment, empowerment and treatment of women in the workplace. At a time when women never voiced their concerns, she was active on the conference circuit, both in Malaysia and internationally, and fought for the position of Malaysian women in the working world. She was also a very sought-after speaker and often the only female speaker at conferences. In the early days, women entering public relations were often trained as a secretary and then placed to do secretarial work (Black, 1976). Paddy was very active in seminars and forums organized for secretaries as the majority were women. In 1972, she spoke at a two-day seminar attended by 100 secretaries from the government and private sectors on the role of secretary and public relations work. According to Paddy, 'a secretary with good relations with people had the foundations for public relations work' (*The Straits Times*, 1972: 9). She described a secretary's work as 'the back-door route to executive positions and one of the spheres where one can aspire to become a PRO ... The way a secretary behaves would reflect the reputation of their company' (*The Straits Times*, 1972: 9).

On another occasion, she was the only woman speaker at a conference for managers, and she emphasized the plight of women managers,

> Women have gained entry to management in Asia, but it is a restricted entry. The real test of woman power is the opportunity for upward mobility and full exposure to planned career development, like inclusion in the deliberate process of making managers ... one thing that Malaysia is not doing very deliberately is and here – east and west come together is making women managers.
> (*The Straits Times*, 1977b: 19)

Paddy has always called on women to pursue an education and qualify for executive positions. She was never hesitant to voice her disapproval of male hegemony. In a talk entitled 'The Brief-Case Women', Paddy blamed male prejudice as a stumbling block against women graduates filling executive positions.

> The male ego also required that a man should dominate a woman in order to prove his superiority. She said male graduates studying along with women acknowledged their academic prowess but graduation viewed the woman as a threat and intrusion into a man's world. Although more and more women are allowed higher education, they are still not given the opportunity to put into practical use their knowledge and training.
>
> (New Nation, 1971)

Conclusion

This chapter has documented Paddy Schubert's 60 years' experience in Malaysian public relations through her memoir, personal interviews and archival sources (newspapers). Fitch (2015) has argued the need for careful interpretation in historical research that identifies public relations 'pioneers' and that relies on personal testimonies and interviews. This research understands Paddy's personal testimonies within the Malaysian historical context and records valuable insights from interviews conducted with those who have worked closely with Paddy. The chapter offers an authentic 'herstory' of Paddy Schubert, as Malaysia's women's PR pioneer, based on hard facts and achievements that Paddy made in enriching the best of the two worlds of public relations – as PR educator and PR practitioner.

During a time when women were seldom working and education was difficult, it is amazing how Paddy, a woman from a small Lancashire town in England with limited exposure to different races, religions and cultures, made her way to a totally different part of the world and succeeded in revolutionizing the position of women in Malaysia.

Paddy's unwavering support for working women is an inspiration to thousands in Malaysia and beyond. Paddy is 95 years old this year. Malaysia today knows her as a prolific writer, a practitioner, a woman who has achieved high positions in a man's world. Adding such women to Malaysia's historical record of public relations gives us a richer understanding of Malaysian public relations.

> You know yourself what you do best and it is advisable to keep focus. For myself, the Good Lord was not over kind- I can't cook, I can't sing, I can't sew and I can't climb Everest. All I do is talk and write. But there is enormous scope for this in the Communications Age.
>
> (Schubert, 2018: 53)

References

Black, S., 1976. *Practical Public Relations*. London: English Language Book Society and Pitman Publishing.

Fitch, K., 2015. Making history: Reflections on memory and elite interviews in public relations research. *Public Relations Inquiry*, 4(2), pp. 131–144.

Fitch, K., 2016. Feminism and public relations. In: J. L'Etang, D. McKie, N. Snow and J. Xifra, ed., *Routledge Handbook of Critical Public Relations*. London: Routledge, pp. 54–64.

Idid, S. A, 2005. *Institute of Public Relations Malaysia*. Kuala Lumpur, Malaysia: International Islamic University Malaysia, pp. 71–80.

Jayasankaran, S., 1999. Fear of the unknown. *Far Eastern Economic Review*, [online] 162(48), p. 19. Available at: <https://search-proquestcom.ezproxy.lib.monash.edu.au/docview/208216529?accountid=12528> [Accessed 23 March 2019].

L'Etang, J., 2015. "It's always been a sexless trade"; "It's clean work"; "There's very little velvet curtain". *Journal of Communication Management*, 19(4), pp. 354–370.

Malaysian Institute of Management, 2018. Management. Special commemorative Issue. [online] Selangor: Malaysian Institute of Management (MIM), pp. 12–20. Available at: <www.mim.org.my/wp-content/uploads/2018/11/28th-TAR-Lecture-Management-Special-edition.pdf>.

New Nation, 1971. Man's ego blamed as bar to women's progress. [online] p. 2. Available at: <https://eresources.nlb.gov.sg/newspapers/Digitised/Article/newnation19710202-> [Accessed 19 April 2020].

Ruhanie, N., 2007. No slowing down for paddy. *Malaysian Business; Kuala Lumpur*, [online] p. 55. Available at: < https://search-proquest-com.ezproxy.lib.monash.edu.au/docview/229706154?accountid=12528> [Accessed 5 April 2020].

Ryan, N., 1965. *The Making of Modern Malaya: A History from Earliest Times to Independence*. 2nd ed. Singapore: Craftsman Press Ltd.

Schubert, P., 2018. *Paddy, A Lifetime of Memories*. Kuala Lumpur: Paddy Schubert Consultants Sdn Bhd.

Souket, R., 2019. *The Early Information Services in British Malaya, 1910–1950: A Historiographical Approach*. Malaysia: International Islamic University Malaysia.

Souket, R. and Idid, S., 2020. The early days of public relations in British Malaya: Winning the hearts and minds of the Empire. *Public Relations Review*, 46(2), p. 101894.

The Star, 2016. Remembering Samantha Schubert. [online] Available at: < www.thestar.com.my/lifestyle/people/2016/04/27/remembering-samantha-schubert/#TzB74hBkDFsjHvuZ.99>.

The Straits Times, 1969. Mrs. Schubert is new trade relations manager of Shell. [online] p. 6. Available at:<https://eresources.nlb.gov.sg/newspapers/Digitised/Article/straitstimes19690415->.

The Straits Times, 1972. A good secretary has all the makings of a PRO. [online] p. 9. Available at: <https://eresources.nlb.gov.sg/newspapers/Digitised/Article/straitstimes19721002->.

The Straits Times, 1977a. 'Women should give full attention to their job and family'. [online] p. 15. Available at: <https://eresources.nlb.gov.sg/newspapers/Digitised/Article/straitstimes19771103->.

The Straits Times, 1977b. Call for more woman execs in Asia. [online] p. 9. Available at: < https://eresources.nlb.gov.sg/newspapers/Digitised/Article/straitstimes19771102->.

8 The Loi Krathong festival and Nang Noppamas
Applying current 'PR' theory to identify the first Thai female PR practitioner

Parichart Sthapitanonda

Introduction

'Loi Krathong' is one of the most-celebrated festivals in Thailand. Each year, the rivers, canals and ponds across Thailand are illuminated with millions of candle-lit 'krathong', small floats in the shape of a lotus flower made from sliced banana stalks and leaves adorned with incense, candles and flowers. According to CNN Travel (2010), Loi Krathong is the world's only festival that lets people send their bad luck, guilt, or negativity, down the river, while paying respect to the river's goddess.

For Thais, Loi Krathong is a cultural event that attracts foreign tourists wanting to watch the spectacle as well as participate in the celebrations with locals. Many have learned about the holiday through tourism advertising, while others have seen the stream of floating Krathong through Hollywood films, such as *The King and I*, which is actually banned in Thailand. For example, the movie includes a beautiful depiction of Loi Krathong, which, with its lotus-shaped floats, has become a symbol of Thai culture or Thainess. In addition, many foreigners experience the festival when they go to dine at local Thai restaurants that have been decorated to mark the celebration.

If you want to understand the symbolism of Loi Krathong and its reflection of Thai culture, it is necessary to turn back the pages to approximately 800 years ago when Nang Noppamas, a concubine of the King of Sukhothai, is credited with creating the lotus-shaped krathong and introducing it to the Thai people along with the festival. Over the years, this holiday has grown in meaning and has come to represent 'Thai-ness' around the world.

Now, if we look at Nang Noppamas from a contemporary public relations perspective, she has implemented what is equivalent to modern PR professionals, who seek to put efforts on promoting 'Thai-ness', the pride of being Thai and the richness of Thai culture that have spread around the globe. Additionally, celebrations of the Loi Krathong event, which was known publicly with Nang Noppamas's story, attract foreign visitors to Thailand in their millions. Moreover, it has introduced them to traditional Thai style and dress, customs and behaviour, along with festive traditions and spirituality, which together co-create a sense of 'Thai-ness'. This 'classical idealism', based on Loi Krathong & Nang Noppmas's story, is then communicated through promotional activities and widely disseminated over a range of media platforms across time.

This article aims to discuss how and why Nang Noppamas could be considered the first Thai female PR practitioner as she exemplifies the roots of public relations well before the term was ever used, or communication technology was well employed to shape public opinion effectively. In order to answer the above questions, I first reviewed the definition of PR as the framework for the analysis, followed by collecting data from the Internet archive and analysis of the results.

Defining PR: from global to local Thai PR professionals

There is a classic parable about blind men and an elephant in Thai, as well as many other cultures. Each of the blind men touch a different part of the elephant and when they compare their findings, they get into an argument about who is correct.

In global public relations, Mary M. Devereux and Ann Pierson-Smith (2008), the authors of *Public Relations in Asia Pacific*, compared descriptions of public relations given by PR academicians and professionals from different places in the world and found that definitions of PR are like the blind men since they had identified different remarks.

Many academics have mentioned that public relations is a combination of art and science (Black and Sharp, 1983). The functionalist school of Public Relations claims that public relations is an obligation of an organization, in which its roles are to establish and manage communication between themselves and the public. In this case, public relations practitioners seek to deliberate plans and principles under actual policies and performance criteria within a specified framework.

Based on the viewpoint of functionalists, public relation practitioners mainly found themselves as 'a representative' of their organizations, operating the flow of information between the organization and their target public. Their works include organizing media events or providing target audiences with news and information about their company, organization or agency. In addition, the functionalists believe the major duties of PR professions relate to management of relationships that can benefit different target or stakeholder groups, including the media. Furthermore, functionalists claim that PR practitioners seek to persuade different target groups to join in different activities of their organization, as well as to develop new activities that will benefit their publics as well as their organizations. These activities include creating mutual understanding and demonstrating their similarities with mutual hopes and their organizations' social concerns. At the same time, they need to manage relations between the agency and publics as well as to manage their corporate image and reputation so that they will be better accepted by society. Recently, the PR roles expanded to include their organization's contribution to sustainable and harmonious development in society.

The critical approach to public relations, on the other hand, looks at public relations as a cultural practice, particularly when it comes to relationship management and trust with stakeholders in various social and cultural contexts. Therefore, they currently recommend PR practitioners with the application of a dialogical approach with the target publics, such as encouraging various stakeholders to define objectives and outcomes at the first stage (i.e. Black & Sharpe, 1983; L'Etang, 2006). With the dialogical approach, the PR practitioners and stakeholders can attain a level of mutual understanding and determine a direction for internal communications, including employee communication and corporate social responsibility's activities that will best benefit society (L'Etang, 2006).

While public relations can be defined or structured by different academics and schools of thought, one common factor is to focus on 'the society' and 'the benefits' to be enjoyed directly or indirectly by each target stakeholder or public.

Retracing public relations in society

The history of public relations can be traced to the industrial revolution, actually coming to fruition in the twentieth century. As nations gained their independence, the private business sectors grew in power, and mass media became more and more influential on peoples' lives.

Many public relations scholars agree that PR began to be recognized as a field in the 1930s with the expansion of major corporations. However, others say that public relations really became important in the 1950s when countries established government press offices and began advertising.

If we conduct a literature review on public relations, we would probably find that the evolution of public relations runs parallel to the history of the United States. L'Etang (2006) observed that the studies by American scholars followed a direction similar to 'the development of innovations introduced to the world by Americans'. Others have examined the development of public relations in, for example, Europe, where they see its advancement in parallel with mass media, as it took on more importance in everyday life.

A number of scholars have adopted a different approach, looking at the growth of public relations in parallel with innovations. They have focused on substance or the essence of public relations, looking at the key issues in different contexts. For example, scholars would analyse how public relations has developed as the world has evolved. As L'Etang (2006) points out, 'PR arises at points of change and over issues where there is disagreement over policy and practice' (p. 31).

When studying the history of public relations, a challenge we face is searching for information about the field before the term 'public relations' was actually coined. Some scholars examine the connection between public relations and the roles of leaders, as well as the influence of 'public thinking', dating as far back as the civilization of Mesopotamia, followed by Assyria, Persia, Egypt, Greece and Rome (Cutlip & Center, 1994; Grunig & Hunt, 1984).

Thailand and Nang Noppamas

Thailand is a Southeast Asian nation, which was known in the past as Siam. The name refers to an ethnic group that was seen to rule over this area of the continent. The earliest recorded history confirms that the Thai nation came into existence with the founding of the kingdom of Sukhothai more than 800 years ago.

While the majority of the population is Buddhist, the people actually adhere to a combination of Buddhist, Hindu and animist beliefs and customs. There has long been a Brahmin caste associated with the monarchy, which is respected, as they are responsible for conducting many of the ceremonies associated with the Royal family.

If the history of public relations in Thailand is aligned with the different monarchs or dynasties that ruled the Kingdom, most Thai scholars would agree that, according to the modern definition for PR, it began around 800 years ago, during the Golden Age of the first Thai Kingdom, Sukhothai.

According to Lapiratanakul (2004), the earliest evidence of ancient PR occurred under King Ramkhamhaeng, which announced the achievements of his reign on stone inscriptions. Other public relations techniques used could be the ringing of a bell hanging above the gate to the palace, acting as a sign for citizen's requests for personal or public consultation with the King. There was also the development of herbal remedies, which would be a learning centre where people can learn how to use herbs to treat different ailments.

In addition to the stories of this great king, there are those of Nang Noppamas, who lived during this same era. While being a commoner, she became known far and wide through her attributed creation of the lotus-shaped krathong, which has served as the symbol for the festival Loi Krathong and as a device that brings all Thai people together when they float their krathong on a waterway. The krathong and this holiday have come to represent Thailand and Thai culture in the purest form, and its festive spectacle has drawn many visitors to the Kingdom to experience the auspicious event (CNN Travel, 2010).

The name Nang (or Mrs.) Noppamas first appears in the ancient book *Tamrap Tao Sri Sutalak* (The Memoires of Tao Sri Sutalak). In modern literary circles, she is known as Nang Noppamas and is considered the first Thai female poet, who wrote that book as her autobiography.

According to the book, Nang Noppamas was born to a Brahmin family, a daughter of Phra Sri Mahosot and Nang Revadee. Her father served as a Brahmin to the Palace of Sukhothai when King Loethai, the son of King Ramkhamhaeng, reigned. Her father taught Noppamas the local language, Buddhism and Hinduism, while her mother trained her in the duty of a woman in daily life. She was then presented to the Palace, when King Luthai, a son of King Loethai, had ascended to the throne. She then became the King's first concubine with the title Tao Sri Chulalak.

Apart from the story of Nang Noppamas, the book provides a combination of prose and poetry as it recalls the founding of Sukhothai. It gives praise to the kings and describes the lifestyles of the people, as well as her life story and presents anecdotes, the proper behaviour of a Thai woman, and the customs and Brahmin ceremonies conducted at court during a 12-month cycle.

Loi Krathong, as it is celebrated today, is a festival discussed as 'Phiti Jawng Prien' (Theological Ceremonies) that is celebrated on the night of a full moon in November. According to the ancient book of Nang Noppamas, she tells how the holiday is one of 12 important ancient ceremonial rites that are celebrated throughout the city on the eve of the full moon of the 12th month of the Thai lunar calendar. Nang Noppamas also describes how the women of the King's Palace, would work together to produce beautifully designed floating, hanging and needle pedestal lanterns to light the evening celebrations.

When we examine Hindu tradition, we find that similar festivities have long been celebrated on the full moon throughout South Asia, and the custom made its way in ancient times to Kingdoms practising Buddhism, like Sukhothai. The release of floating lanterns and floats then became a mixture of Buddhist and Hindu beliefs. For the Thais, these were seen as acts of paying homage to the 'Footprint' of the Lord Buddha found on the bank of the Narmada River that flows in central India, considered the source of Hindu mythology. At the same time, these offerings are made as an apology and to appease the goddess Mae Khongkha (Ganges), who provides the water needed for nourishment and sustenance, which people use for disposing of their waste. It is also believed that people could pray and send their bad luck, guilt and negativity flow with the krathong so that they can enjoy a healthier life after completing the ceremony.

In the old days, the palace would organize a boat procession and ceremonies, which would include the release of a krathong decorated with flowers, incense and candles upon the rivers and waterways throughout the capital.

These celebrations were held just five days after Nang Noppamas began to reside in the palace. Nang Noppamas was able to demonstrate her ability to create and construct a new design of floating lanterns in the shape of blooming lotus flowers, which attracted much attention as they were so much more impressive than the old wooden floats that had been used in the past. She conveyed the meaning behind her krathong to the King.

Her persuasive message was so strong. She did this by saying:

> Your Majesty, on this the eve of the full moon of the 12th lunar month festivities, the lotus flowers blossom under its heavenly light like the flowers do when they feel the rays of the sun. As your humble servant, I have made a floating lantern in the shape of the lotus found along the banks of the Narmada River that decorate the holy footprint of the Lord Buddha.

The persuasive explanation of Nang Noppamas reflects the essence of communication as the lotus-shaped krathong symbolized the people's spiritual beliefs. Therefore, following her explanation, the King adopted Nang Noppamas' symbolic float and issued the following decree:

From this day forth, on the eve of the full moon of the 12th lunar month, floating lanterns will be released in the shape of a blooming lotus following the design of Nang Noppamas as an offering to the footprint of the Lord Buddha located on the bank of the Naramada River.

Since that time, approximately 800 years, the lotus-shaped krathong and the name Nang Noppamas remain a deep-rooted part of Thai culture, and the holiday Loi Krathong is still celebrated annually on the eve of the full moon of the 12th Thai lunar month throughout Thailand.

Nang Noppamas: fact or fiction?

Generally, Thais believe that Nang Noppamas was an actual person who was very talented. However, much discussion still takes place regarding the veracity of the origin, particularly as this story has its roots in the earliest Thai oral history, little of which was later recorded.

Thailand entered its literary 'Golden Age' after the founding of the fourth Thai Kingdom, Rattanakosin, with Bangkok, or Krung Thep (City of Angels), as the capital, once the kingdom felt safe and stable following the fall of Ayutthaya. Members of the Royal family then wrote literary works that were distributed among the populace. A society of scholars and experts emerged who devoted themselves to editing or producing a body of knowledge to reproduce what had been lost with the ransacking and destruction of Ayutthaya by the Burmese in 1767.

When Westerners introduced printing technology to Thailand approximately 100 years ago, printers and publishers were established to produce newspapers, leaflets and books. At the same time, the Thai government began to print its own materials for distribution. The Thai PR scholar, Napawan Tantivejakul (2014), pointed out that King Mongkut (Rama IV) even before this was the first to see the importance of disseminating law and regulatory notifications and had established the 'Royal Thai Government Gazette'.

With the advancement of technology, more news and information could be released in the Kingdom among the literate populace, and, thus, printed materials became the symbol of modernity and wealth among the new generation. The Government then turned to producing books on religion, such as the Buddhist Tripitika or Pali Canon, books on medicinal herbs, biographies and discourses by important personages of the past, as well as literary works and philosophy for wide distribution.

In addition to printing government documents, it became popular among the aristocratic sector of society to print Funeral Books that would be distributed among those who attended a wake and cremation. These would include important facts or thoughts that the family wanted to disseminate as a form of public relations. Therefore, the book by Nang Noppamas, *The Memoires of Tao Sri Chulalak*, was produced as a funeral book in 1914 for the funeral of one of King Mongkut's consorts.

Since that time, there has been continual debate about the authenticity of the book because of the Foreword, written by Prince Damrong, a relative of the deceased, historian and government official of high rank. This appears to say the book was actually written during the formative years of the Rattanakosin Kingdom, approximately 100 years earlier, and not more than 700 years before the time of his writing.

Prince Damrong's argument is that Nang Noppamas mentions in the text a foreign visitor from the West, an American; however, at the time she lived, America had not been established. Prince Damrong further observes that the writing describes the lifestyle of the time quite realistically and that this style did not become popular in Thai writing until Westerners began to visit the Kingdom. At the time it was supposed to have been written, he says the style was much more idealistic when describing life and society.

Even with this argument that Nang Noppamas never really existed or that the book, *The Memories of Tao Sri Chulalak*, was actually written during the early nineteenth century, it is accepted that Sukhothai is located in a barren plain that needed dams or reservoirs constructed to accumulate and conserve water. Water would thus have been highly valued, while in other areas where the water flowed and was readily available for consumption and agriculture, there probably would have been less inclination to conduct ceremonies, like Loi Krathong, to pay homage to the spirits for this precious gift.

Meanwhile, another school of thought among Thai historians states that Nang Noppamas did actually live for the following reasons. Firstly, her name is written on the stone inscriptions of Ramkhamhaeng, and this shows she was an important personage during that period. In addition, the story of Nang Noppamas has an important place in Thai oral history.

Regarding her book, 'The Memoires of Tao Sri Chulalak', it could have been altered during transcriptions because the earliest texts were written on palm leaf and then transcribed, over time, onto paper and then produced as a book. Over the centuries, the texts could also have become damaged and partly destroyed, particularly during the wars between the Thais and Burmese. Therefore, it would not have been until after the fall of Ayutthaya and the founding of Bangkok that a final version could have been produced.

Whatever the case, this school of historians will accept that even if this history has been revised, those in power wanted to tell a story of a beautiful, virtuous woman who was a member of the ruling class of that time. She would represent the ideal Thai woman, one who looks after and cares for her parents and is a devoted wife who assists her husband in all his endeavours, as well as caring for her children and ensuring they study hard. This has merit according to the Buddhist faith, and, finally, it follows the example of Tao Sri Chulalak.

Nang Noppamas: reborn through promotions and contests

While the debate continues among Thai historians as to whether Nang Noppamas ever really existed or is just a story used to communicate a message, the viewpoint of Thai society also needs to be considered as they continue to admire this woman and credit her with the creation of the lotus-shaped krathong used to celebrate the holiday.

Many historical texts discuss Loi Krathong and tell how the holiday has been celebrated by the different Thai kingdoms and dynasties up to the present day. They describe how, after Bangkok was established as the kingdom's capital, the monarchs and their families, as well as vassals, would produce very large and ornate lotus-shaped krathongs and hold competitions to determine the most beautiful. At other times, they would replace the krathongs with floats of candle lanterns forming a likeness of Nang Noppamas.

From 1950 to the present day, Loi Krathong and Nang Noppamas have been promoted and grown in importance. Private Royal ceremonies have been conducted annually, and pictures of His Majesty and his family releasing their krathongs in the Chao Phraya River have always been printed on the front page of all newspapers or broadcast on television. In addition, stories have been released in the news in some years about a lucky person who found the krathong released by H. M. the King. They would then keep and cherish this krathong, as they believe it can bring them good fortune.

As interest in the holiday grew and celebrations became more lavish and elaborate, it became an important vehicle for promoting tourism. In fact, the city of Chiang Mai promoted celebrations in 1948 that included the release of floating lanterns in addition to krathongs. Then, in 1969, the Chiang Mai provincial administration joined with the National Tourism Office to organize activities to celebrate Loi Krathong in the waterways, as it had been celebrated in the ancient Thai capital. These festivities included a procession displaying many krathongs, as well as a Chiang Mai Nang Noppamas beauty pageant as highlights of the celebrations. They also invited members of the media to join in the fun and help promote the events and create interest in the beauty pageant and its contestants.

One cultural historian, when interviewed about the Nang Noppamas beauty pageant in Chiang Mai, said,

> At first, the parade of krathongs and Nang Noppamas attracted a large audience and the contestants would be dressed in local traditional costumes. They would possibly carry a krathong or candle and incense across the stage so the judges could see their faces. This was around 1969 to 1970 and, while the crowds were large, they were quite quiet and well-behaved.
>
> The historian went on to say, while discussing the popularity of the event, the stage for the old day's pageant was quite simple, nothing like the popularity of the current event in the 21st century. The crowds of those days would wait patiently even though the contest would be over rather quickly. They would see the contestants and the crowning of the winner, and that was enough to make them happy.

Nang Noppamas: symbol of aristocratic and contemporary femininity

Today, Nang Noppamas has become a symbol for Thai female nobility. Many Thai girls born on Loi Krathong have been named Noppamas; at the same time, many Thai girls dream of winning a Nang Noppamas beauty pageant as they grow up.

The Tourism Authority of Thailand (TAT) has used Nang Noppamas and Loi Krathong to promote Thailand as a tourist destination. This has been especially true since 1990 when they launched their global campaign, 'Amazing Thailand', with pictures of a Thai woman dressed as Nang Noppamas to represent Thai women in their promotional materials for Thailand and its ancient historical landmarks. In addition to print and television advertising, TAT collaborates with different organizations to promote Loi Krathong celebrations and Nang Noppamas processions at ancient sites, such as the Sukhothai Historical Park, where it is believed Nang Noppamas first created her lotus-shaped krathong and promoted the festivities. These celebrations would also be broadcast live on nationwide Thai television.

In addition, government agencies, local organizations, schools and businesses contribute to decorating the Nang Noppamas Pageant festival stage or parade, particularly at the more popular venues, as well as along the Chao Phraya River banks, public parks, schools and universities, shopping centres and communities. It has been estimated that there will be well over 100 major festivals with entertainment stages and activities organized around the country during an annual celebration.

Today, the contestants for the Nang Noppamas pageants are, for the most part, students sponsored by different organizations.

> Today, contestants must prepare themselves well for the pageants, which means having massages and skincare treatments, much like a young woman would do if she entered a national beauty contest.

The contestants now, in addition to competing in traditional costume, must answer questions or perform to demonstrate just why they should be selected to represent Nang Noppamas. The judges consider many attributes, including the contestant's appearance, her eyes, smile and figure, hairstyle and complexion, poise, posture and walk, as well as her behaviour and intelligence when interviewed.

> She has to be a housewife who is good at doing her tasks. She should be charming, speak sweetly and demonstrate inventiveness. She should be bright and intelligent as well as have the ability to promote the event and serve as a representative for the province if selected to be Nang Noppamas.

The above quote is how one historian described Noppamas, but many contests and processions confine their participants today to students or different age groups. These begin with Nu Noi Noppamas (Young Noppamas) for young girls, followed by school and university Nang Noppamas beauty contests, provincial competitions and even Golden Age Nang Noppamas pageants held for residents in elderly housing. There are also Nang Noppamas contests held in prisons and for transvestites, transsexuals and transgenders that add to the celebrations and provide a chance for many of different ages, backgrounds and circumstances to fulfil their dream to be Nang Noppamas.

One local scholar conducted a survey on the reasons why a Thai woman would want to be Nang Noppamas. They found that it is because Nang Noppamas represents the ideal Thai woman, who is beautiful, with an attractive figure and glowing skin. She is intelligent and well educated and has impressive manners, presenting an image that is a blend of classical-contemporary Thai.

Furthermore, Nang Noppamas represents Thai customs and traditions that must be preserved. She provides promotional opportunities that can make people aware of the 'richness of Thai culture' through public relations activities. Nang Noppamas represents the ideal noble Thai woman of the Kingdom of Sukhothai, the first Thai capital.

Therefore, it is not surprising that a woman considered the Kingdom's most beautiful was a past winner of a Nang Noppamas beauty pageant before pursuing the Miss Thailand and Miss Universe crowns.

Immortal Nang Noppamas in the digital age

The birth of the Internet brought many changes and challenges with the advent of this digital age, raising questions as to how it would affect Nang Noppamas. Would she grow in importance or be forgotten over time?

A Google search (June 2016) found as many as 225,000 listings in Thai concerning Nang Noppamas and 136,000 entries in English (in 0.65 s). In addition, if one searched on the Internet for organizations promoting and publicizing Nang Noppamas beauty contests, sites designed to attract audiences would be found. A number of websites have launched the announcement of their contest dates, the lists of requirements for contestants, information for anyone wanting to participate and the prizes for the winners. They would also have photographs of the winners and runners up, along with the award ceremonies as well as short video clips that may also be uploaded onto YouTube or similar sites.

If, on the other hand, one was to examine the interest of Internet users, whether conducting a search in English or Thai, a word search for Nang Noppamas, Loy Krathong and Nang Noppamas Beauty Contest would be used. However, in the Thai social context, digital communication still conveys the same characteristics for Nang Noppamas and what she represents, the ideal classical-contemporary Thai woman.

For example, our analysis of searches on the Internet found that Thai users were interested in finding a large amount of information about Nang Noppamas beauty contests, particularly concerning appearance and dress. They want to know what style of costume a contestant should wear and whether they can be rented and, if so, where. They also want to know how to prepare and what the judges would be looking for.

Of special interest are the questions contestants are asked. Those thinking of participating want to prepare and answer queries in a manner expected of Nang Noppamas. They would be asked how Nang Noppamas today, or a modern Nang Noppamas, would help to preserve Thai culture, protect the environment or feel about love and sexual relations.

Nang Noppamas: Is she the first Thai female PR practitioner?

It is a big challenge to claim that Nang Noppamas is the first Thai female PR practitioner. In order to get a clear picture, a table showing a comparison of Nang Noppamas's roles and the definition of PR is provided.

According to the above table, whether Nang Noppamas is the first Thai female PR is partly dependent on the ways people perceive the concept of public relations. For example, if public relations is defined as a strategic communication process to educate and inform the public, then the actions taken concerning Nang Noppamas are quite clever when it comes to anticipating and interpreting public opinions. The annual celebrations that take place on the full moon of the 12th month of the Thai lunar calendar help to communicate love for the environment

Table 8.1 A Comparison of PR's Definitions and Nang Noppamas' PR Achievement

Definitions of PR	*Nang Noppamas' PR Achievement*
PR as the engagement with stakeholders	Nang Noppamas' ability to build closer ties between many different publics.
PR as the message management	Nang Noppamas' life & works are easily recognized by WOM, e-WOM from generation to generation.
PR as putting things into action and looking for the results	The celebrating festival, and the potentials to gain supports and sponsors of Nang Noppamas' beauty pageants.
PR effect as the number of people who engage in the projects	The holiday festivities still attract the Thai populace as well as international visitors. And Nang Noppamas' beauty pageants are still a major event.
PR impact as the extent to which the key message long last.	The acts of Nang Noppamas were quite successful as she and her event - Loy Kratong - are still important 800 years after she was credited with creating the first lotus-shapes kratong and promoting the Loi Krathong festival.
PR impact as the positive reflection across centuries	Nang Noppamas is still considered an important historical figure and still has an influence on society

and spirituality. At the same time, Nang Noppamas is considered the creator of the lotus-shaped krathong, which serves as a communication device, that is, a symbol that is easily understood and can be engaged with because people today will produce krathongs in similar lotus-shaped likenesses.

If public relations is concerned with efforts to influence or change public policy, Nang Noppamas can be applied to analyse target publics and to develop the best messages to accomplish practitioners' goals. In the past, it was believed that Nang Noppamas could explain to her King the meaning of the lotus-shaped krathong and convince him to adopt her idea and announce that everyone should also adopt this style of krathong for the festival.

If the purpose of public relations is to encourage public acceptance of what to do and what not to do, Nang Noppamas was a smart person to use the book as a communication device to educate local Thais about Thai femininity, Thai religion, the Thai monarchy and even how parents should raise their children. These messages, which are conveyed in the original memoires of Nang Noppamas, have become the 'strong' message for Thai women to follow from generation to generation.

If public relations is based on engagement with stakeholders, then the activities of Loi Krathong help to build closer ties between many different publics. The story of Nang Noppamas provides a key message that is easily communicated by word-of-mouth from one generation to the next. This has created a powerful force for those who want to support and sponsor Nang Noppamas and her message of Thainess and femininity, even if many of the descriptions in the memoire she is credited with writing have been forgotten.

If the success of a public relations campaign is measured by how much people talk about it, then the acts of Nang Noppamas were quite successful as she and Loy Krathong are still important 800 years after she is credited with creating the first lotus-shaped krathong and promoting the Loi Krathong festival. She is still considered an important historical figure and remains an influence on society. The holiday festivities still attract the Thai populace as well as international visitors and the Nang Noppamas beauty pageants are still a major event.

Conclusion

If the power of public relations is in the management of relations with target publics, the results of the public relations styles used by Nang Noppamas are substantial evidence demonstrated by different communication channels and vehicles each day. Especially, her influence on relationship management can be recognized by the level of Thai awareness of the contributions that Nang Noppamas has made to society and the environment. What can be seen is even the small activities can influence making the world appear beautiful. She serves as a symbol that influences people to be more socially and environmentally responsible, and the public relations activities associated with Nang Noppamas and Loi Krathong strongly communicate what is meant by Thainess in a way that is understandable, memorable and sustainable.

While the debate continues as to whether Nang Noppamas lived many centuries ago and wrote her 'Memoires of Tao Sri Chulalak' or not, it still can be said that she is seen as the embodiment of true Thai femininity and beauty, which is reflected in the lotus-shaped krathong and holiday celebrations she is credited with creating.

So, what do you think? Should she be recognized as the first female PR practitioner in Thai history?

References

Black, S., and Sharpe, M. L. (1983). *Practical public relations*. New Jersey: Prentice-Hall.
CNN Travel. (2010). The ultimate guide to Loy Krathong. Available at http://travel.cnn.com/bangkok/visit/ultimate-guide-loy-krathong-823312/ (Accessed on 10 May 2020).
Cutlip, S. M., Center, A., and Broom, G. M. (1994). *Effective Public Relations* (7th edn). Horlow: Prentice Hall.
Devereux, M. M., and Pierson-Smith, A. (2008). *Public Relations in Asia Pacific: Communicating Effectively Across Cultures*. Singapore: John Wiley & Sons (Asia).
Ekachai, D. (1994). Public relations and teaching in Thailand. Paper presented at the Annual Meeting of the Speech Communication Association. New Orleans, LA, November, 19–22. Available at http://files.eric.ed.gov/fulltext/ED384092.pdf (Accessed on 10 May 2020).
Grunig, J., and Hunt, T. (1984). *Managing Public Relations*. New York: Holt, Rinehart & Winston.
L'Etang, J. (2006). *Public Relations: Concepts, Practice and Critique*. London: Sage.
Lapiratanakul, V. (2006). *Public Relations* (11th edn). Thailand: Chulalongkorn University Press.
Tantivejakul, N. (2014). The public relations communication during the reign of King Rama IV, *Journal of Public Relations and Advertising*, 7 (1), pp. 12–37.

9 Inez Kaiser
The perseverance of a public relations pioneer

Denise Hill and Shelley Spector

Introduction

Although there is a dearth of women in US public relations history, a number of scholars have closed this gap with research on female public relations practitioners and those not considered 'PR people' but whose work involved developing and implementing public relations tactics. Despite women now being included in history sections of public relations textbooks, their contributions are often limited to a paragraph. As a result, students, scholars and practitioners know little of the work they did. Instead, the field's history continues to be dominated by a 'great man perspective'; specifically, a 'great White man'. If women were overlooked, minorities were completely excluded. While this exclusion is slowly being addressed with the acknowledgement of African-American practitioners, such as Moss Kendrix, Joseph Baker and Ofield Dukes, women of colour have been rendered non-existent. In the few instances a Black woman is mentioned, that woman is the public relations pioneer Inez Kaiser. Kaiser founded her eponymous PR agency in 1957. Not only was Kaiser the first African-American woman to open her own PR firm, she was also the first to serve national clients. However, beyond a few sentences in textbooks, Inez Kaiser's contributions have not been studied; therefore, this chapter is the first published overview of Kaiser's career as PR pioneer and civic leader.

Literature

Pamela Creedon (1989) wrote that the recorded history of women in public relations failed to capture adequately the contributions of the few women included. Marilyn Kern Foxworth (1989) found the same results in her examination of public relations textbooks published from 1979 to 1988. She found that there was a void in women's contributions overall, and that most books ignored women's roles in public relations history (ibid.: 34). In a similar study, Kern-Foxworth (1990) examined minority representation in public relations textbooks in the same timeframe. She found that only 0.7 percent of the pages in the 60 books she examined included information about people of colour who were currently practicing, and most of the books ignored the contributions of minority practitioners to public relations history. Twenty years later, a similar study by Sandra Wills Hannon found little had changed. According to Creedon, 'Women's contributions over the past 80 years usually merit about a paragraph in the average textbook' (2004: 224).

Brigitta Bruner's (2006) examination of introductory public relations textbooks found that men continued to be featured more prominently than women, although she did not specifically explore public relations history chapters. Melody Fisher's (2018) study of minority public relations pioneers in public relations textbooks from 1995 to 2018 found improvement over previous related research, with Doris Fleischman, Moss Kendrix and Betsy Plank recognized as pioneers. Fisher concluded that although the quality of information about minorities increased since previous studies, the number of minorities included could be greatly improved.

In a historiography of North American public relations, Karla Gower (2017) wrote that US public relations history has been a history of men in public relations, centred on Edward Bernays and Ivy Lee, both of whom are often dubbed the fathers of public relations. While Gower notes that this 'great man perspective' has resulted in an emphasis on corporate public relations, it is essential to recognize that men of colour have been omitted from the narrative, regardless of the type of public relations they practiced. This is largely due to the fact that public relations historians presumed there were no minority public relations pioneers (see Cutlip 1994: xi).

Despite the increasing attention to women's contributions to public relations history, there is no woman who is recognized as the mother of public relations. The reason may be, as Karen Miller Russell (1997) notes, few women worked in formal public relations during the early decades of modern public relations. However, in her examination of women's roles in public relations from 1940 to 1970, J. Suzanne Horsley (2009) found that despite their contributions being excluded or minimized, women played very active roles in the public relations profession.

The woman most often studied is Doris Fleischman. Susan Henry (1997, 1998, 1999), who has written extensively on Fleischman, noted that Fleischman and her husband Edward Bernays were equal partners in the firm Edward L. Bernays, Counsel on Public Relations, which was 'one of the country's premier agencies; they operated from the 1920s to the 1950s' (1997: 51). While Bernays is often labelled a father of public relations, Fleischman has not been dubbed the female equivalent despite their equal partnership. Lamme (2001) speculates that the reasons why so little has been written about Fleischman in comparison to Bernays include Fleischman's behind-the-scenes role and her possible desire for a lower profile. Further, unlike Bernays, Fleischman did not view her life's mission to be public relations (Lamme: 14). However, according to Lamme (2007), Fleischman saw herself just as much of a pioneer as Bernays was, albeit without his self-promotion.

Scholars have begun to identify and research other pioneering women. Although they practiced decades after the early days of Bernays and Lee, their contributions deserve recognition. Karen Miller (1997) profiled Jane Stewart, a public relations executive with a consulting firm that later became a Hill & Knowlton subsidiary. Martinelli and Toth (2010) examined the career of Charlotte Klein, who began her 50-year public relations career in 1947 as a publicist for the film industry and later worked in agency PR. Natalia Rodríguez-Salcedo and Beatriz Gómez-Baceiredo (2017) explored Teresa Dorn's work from 1974 to 1995 when she was instrumental in establishing Burson-Marsteller branch offices in Madrid and Barcelona.

In addition, a number of women were practicing public relations as part of their work affecting social change, although it was not named as such. For example, one of the public relations strategies Ida B. Wells used in her anti-lynching campaign was to draw foreign attention to the atrocities happening in the United States (Ward-Johnson, 2006). Tactically, she gave speeches in England that provided stark detail on the problem. Other women, including birth control activist, Margaret Sanger, and Frances Willard, president of the Women's Christian Temperance Union, used public relations in advocating reform (see Straughan 2007).

In a study of workforce diversity research, Vardeman-Winter and Place found that the 'standard, White, heterosexual, American experience' was overrepresented in the PR industry (2017: 326). Although this research focused on workforce issues, it highlights a pattern of exclusion in a number of areas of public relations, from history, to practitioners and academics in the workforce, to academic research. While scholars have begun to address the lack of women in public relations history, research specifically on the lack of minority women in public relations history has been rare. Although her name is now included in some public relations textbooks (see, for example, Teruggi Page and Parnell 2019: 41 and Broom and Sha 2013: 96), there have been no detailed studies of Inez Kaiser and her public relations career. Through an examination of historical documents and interviews with Kaiser and her son, this chapter provides a look at the career of Inez Kaiser and its impact on both the industry and mid-twentieth century society.

Inez Kaiser: background

Inez Kaiser was born in April 1918 in Kansas City, Kansas. She graduated from the segregated Sumner High School in 1935, where she was in the top 10 percent of her class. She then attended Kansas Junior College, graduating in 1937, in the top 5 percent of her class (Kaiser Personal Background promotional flyer n.d.).

Kaiser achieved a bachelor's degree in home economics from Kansas State Teachers College in Pittsburg, Kansas and a master's degree in home economics from Columbia University. Furthermore, she was awarded an honorary doctor of law degree from Lincoln University in Jefferson City, Missouri, for her contributions in home economics in the public schools of Missouri and for her achievements in public relations. In addressing some of the racial discrimination she faced, Kaiser recalled an incident in an undergraduate cooking class in which the Black students were not allowed to cook, saying 'all we did was watch the White girls cook' (Kaiser 2015).

After graduating, Kaiser was a school teacher in Kansas City, Kansas for four years; she later taught high-school home economics in Kansas City, Missouri for thirteen years. While still teaching, Kaiser parlayed her love of writing into a newspaper column, 'Fashionwise and Otherwise'. Her column originally ran in one Black newspaper and was later syndicated to Black newspapers around the country. For her column, she travelled to Fashion Press Week events in New York, California and Europe, as well as to fashion shows in Paris, making valuable contacts along the way (Kaiser 'Fashionwise and Otherwise' promotional flyer n.d. and Patrick 2010). Kaiser also wrote a column 'Hints for Homemakers' and a column for Sears about shopping in that store.

Kaiser's friend, Howard Wood, editor and publisher of a local Black newspaper, the *St. Louis Argos*, had suggested that Inez should get into public relations. Kaiser later remarked that, at the time, she had not heard of public relations, although she had been practicing it, most likely, through some of her newspaper work (Kaiser 2015). She did not immediately take Wood's suggestion, and it was only after Kaiser grew disenchanted with teaching and quit her job that she opened Inez Kaiser & Associates in 1957. As a new business owner, she wanted to secure office space in downtown Kansas City but building owners did not want Black tenants. After six weeks of trying and only after threatening to call the Presidents of NBC, CBS and ABC, whom she knew from working on her newspaper column, Kaiser opened an office in downtown Kansas City, Missouri, in the City National Bank building. Her tenancy marks one of her many firsts: Hers was the first Black-owned firm in downtown Kansas City.

Kaiser's focus and determination were evident in how she approached her new venture. Instead of first obtaining clients and then securing office space, she did the opposite. She contacted a number of businesses who acknowledged her qualifications but still did not hire her. Despite being discouraged, she persevered and finally landed Jenkins Music Company as her first account. She later branched into national work, acquiring the Lever Brothers account. That work led to her firm becoming a consultant to J. Walter Thompson on its 7Up account. Over the course of her career, she represented such companies as Sterling Drug, Adolph Coors Company, Burger King Corporation, Transworld Airlines, The Pillsbury Company, Standard Brands, Sperry and Hutchinson Company, Southwestern Bell Telephone Company and Sears Roebuck & Company. In addition to local and national leadership and service roles she held in numerous organizations focused on equal opportunity for minorities, she also worked with the National Association for the Advancement of Colored People (NAACP), the National Urban League and the Congressional Black Caucus on behalf of her clients (Kaiser Capabilities Statements n.d.).

Kaiser started her agency at a time when business interest in the Black consumer was on the rise. Prior to World War II, African-Americans had been relegated to a role in society that resulted in marketers ignoring them as potential consumers. After the war, with improved economic conditions for many Americans and increased activities that gave rise to the modern civil rights movement, businesses began to recognize the value of the African-American consumer (Foster Davis 2013). In a 1943 research report about African-American purchasing power, Kansas City, Missouri was among the '50 cities leading in Negro population' (Sullivan 1945). A 1952 (Keysor) article in *Commerce* magazine outlined how to reach the $15 million Negro market. That same year, *Tide*, the newsmagazine of sales and advertising, highlighted how advertisers could reach this growing Black population (The Negro Market, 1952). Proponents of the Black consumer marketplace conducted research providing data to support the spending power of African-Americans. One large advertising agency, Batten Barton Durstine and Osborn, created an Ethnic Markets division, headed by an African-American advertising executive (Foster Davis 2013: 481). Although it did not create a separate division, J. Walter Thompson (JWT) hired Black marketing consultants, such as Kaiser, to reach Black consumers.

Kaiser's promotional material suggested she was poised to take advantage of the Black market, and she presented herself as an expert in reaching it. With a headline 'Step in the profitable Negro market with Inez Kaiser', she listed sales promotions, conventions, trade shows, market research, market consultant, public relations and surveys as services she could provide (Kaiser 'Step into the Profitable Negro Market' n.d.).

Her services were available in the following fields:

1. Fashions: Women, Men and Children
2. Food and Beverages
3. Home Furnishings and other Commodities

Her focus on those fields indicated she combined her home economics background with public relations to obtain and serve clients (see Horsley 2009:112). She also noted she could provide these services to 'manufacturers, utilities, industries and retailers', and she would do so using all media, including 'TV, newspapers, magazines, radio and direct mail' (Kaiser ibid.).

Kaiser was specific regarding her expertise in reaching Black consumers. Among the work and results she could achieve for her potential clients, her promotional material includes:

> Increase your profits;
> Serve as an interpretive arm for the ethnic market;
> Project the image of your product directly to Negro consumers;
> Market your product through the press, radio and television;
> Plan promotions with key Negro organizations at conventions and home shows;
> Conduct surveys and market research;
> Make the Negro market conscious of your brand name;

Do a public relations job;
Create good community and public relations with Negro consumers
(Kaiser Company Backgrounder Promotional Flyer).

Kaiser later remarked, 'My role was to convince Black people to buy different products and services' (Kaiser 2015).

Convince them she did. While Kaiser was not the only African-American public relations or marketing expert in the post-war era, she was the only African-American *woman*. With women making up to 80 percent of household purchases (Berthiaune 2013), who better than another woman to know how to win the hearts and minds of America's most important consumers?

During the time her fledging public relations business in Kansas City was beginning to take off, Kaiser's decision to publish a cookbook brought her name to national attention. In 1960, Kaiser wrote up her traditional set of family recipes, passed down from generations, in a book she called *Soul Food Cookery*. While it was not the nation's first cookbook featuring Southern recipes, it was the first to describe it as 'Soul Food' (Liberman 2011: 165), thus introducing a new cuisine into White American culture and popularizing a once Black-only phrase into the American vernacular. Kaiser later remarked that although she had trademarked the name 'Soul Food Cookery', in hindsight she should have trademarked the name 'soul food' (Kaiser 2015). So popular was the book – it had three printings – that she was invited to be a guest on the *Today Show*, where she explained to Barbara Walters how to cook fried okra, pig's feet and collard greens (Today Show photo 1968). In a press release announcing the third edition of the book, she explained that it was 'written with the hope that it will help bridge the racial gap by understanding through one of life's basic needs – food' (News from Inez press release, n.d.).

The back cover of *Soul Food Cookery* (1968) contains a dozen excerpts of enthusiastic reviews from major mainstream newspapers. For example:

> 'The time is ripe for "Soul Food" ', from the *Chicago Sun Times*;
> 'Soul Food is great for the tummy', from the *Des Moines Register Tribune*;
> 'Once a man gets emotional about his food, it is worth a million to him, even if it costs only seven cents to prepare' and 'Low-income housewives who don't have their grandmother's cooking talents will consult [this] book', from the *Houston Chronicle*.

The cookbook managed to catapult Kaiser's national popularity, not only with the nation's top food editors as her name also came to the attention of Madison Avenue.

In the early Sixties, she was contacted by J. Walter Thompson to handle the 7Up account as a special market consultant, 'the first Black consultant to the world's largest advertising agency' (Kaiser Capabilities Statements, n.d.). Kaiser was charged with instructing bottlers on how to 'get a larger share of the Black dollar' (ibid.).

Kaiser headed a number of projects, including writing a marketing manual about the Black consumer for use by 7Up bottlers nationwide. Kaiser also launched community relations programmes for the brand, including 7Up-branded workshops for hundreds of high-school students in Los Angeles and Philadelphia, with a hope of stimulating their interest in mass communications (ibid.).

In 1968, a vice president of J. Walter Thompson Company wrote a letter commending Kaiser for her public relations skills, 'particularly in the area of Negro market development ... Her contacts and acceptance among top leaders in the Negro community are exceptional' (Loken 1968).

Ogilvy and Mather also contacted her in the Sixties to work on public relations for the Lever Brothers Company and its numerous brands. The initial assignment was to produce 'editorial advertising (what would today be called 'sponsored content') in the newspapers reaching Black communities across the country. She created a monthly 'Hints for Homemakers', an advice column that ran nationwide in 26 newspapers. In the columns, Kaiser offered advice to 'readers' about remedying their dry skin, bad breath or greasy, oily stains (Kaiser Capabilities Statements). Written with warmth and authority, the columns always managed to cite a Lever Brothers' product as the solution.

A letter to Kaiser from a Lever Brothers community relations manager in 1964 demonstrated the impact of these advice columns. He reported on a meeting he had with the editor and publisher of the *Chicago Defender*, one of the nation's oldest and most influential Black newspapers. 'We talked about you and your column, among other things, and he had some good compliments to pay you. He thought the column was excellent and he felt sure the readers would find it a most helpful shopping guide' (Gerz 1964).

Kaiser also wrote an advice column for Sears Roebuck & Co. In 'Shopping Sears with Inez', she subtly promoted Sears' goods, from furniture to fashion. In her capabilities brochure, she stressed that the 'editorial approach was used instead of display ads because of its appeal to Black readers' (Kaiser Capabilities Statements).

For Sterling Drug, Kaiser sought to position it as the one pharmaceutical company that uniquely understood the needs of the Black market and truly cared about the health and well-being of Black communities. Kaiser arranged for Sterling sales representatives to hold receptions for Black leaders at the annual conventions of the NAACP and the National Urban League. She also convinced the company to donate money to educational scholarships, such as through the United Negro College Fund and several community scholarship programmes in local Black communities around the country (Kaiser Capabilities Statements).

While Kaiser's early focus was promoting consumer brands, her later focus included promoting equal rights, especially for minority business owners. Her trajectory from publicist to activist is documented first-hand in the speeches, invitations, photographs and White House memoranda in her archives.

A registered Republican, Kaiser first got involved in national business issues during the Nixon Administration. In 1972, she was selected to head a federally sponsored programme to study the role of minority women in the economy. Her unsurprising findings showed women and minorities were relegated to lower pay grades and were provided no upward mobility. To help provide greater opportunities for minority women, she founded the National Association of Minority Women in Business, which, at its height, had more than 5000 members across the nation (Kaiser 1998).

Under this Association, Kaiser coordinated and conducted conferences, seminars, workshops and sensitivity training for top management and junior-level employees alike, instructing them on how to best work with minorities and women employees. The goal was to bring about increased interpersonal understanding and support for Equal Employment Opportunity (EEO). These conferences helped provide an understanding of the experience of minority workers and acceptance of cultural differences, offering problem-solving strategies about recruiting, hiring and career development. Some of the conferences included workshops in mass communications, careers for high-school girls and how best to deal with hunger, which were directed to low-income families; there was also a public relations and communications workshop. All these workshops and conferences came under Kaiser's label: 'Black Is Now! Black Is Profit! Black Is Here to Stay!' (Kaiser Capabilities Statements).

For the Small Business Administration, Kaiser conducted a study in a four-state area, revealing a need for basic business education in market research and business management among minority business owners. This resulted in a seminar, 'Think Big, Think Positive, Act, and Be Successful', aimed to help them develop the tools they needed to start and manage a successful business venture (ibid.).

Her work on behalf of minority businesses was noticed by the White House administration, and she received an official invitation in 1972 to 'attend and participate in the inauguration of Richard Milhous Nixon and Spiro Theodore Agnew' (Invitation 1972).

Kaiser was a frequent visitor to Washington, D.C.; in many cases, at the official invitation of the White House. For instance, a 1981 memorandum on White House stationery from Elizabeth Dole (named as 'public liaison' by Pres. Reagan) is addressed to 'Leaders from the Small Business Community' (Dole 1981). It lists one man or woman representing each State of the Union, with Kaiser's name included under 'Missouri'. It cited Kaiser as representing the National Association of Minority Women in Business. The Administration's representatives invited to the meeting included Secretary of Commerce, Malcolm Baldridge, Jr., and Secretary of the Treasury, Donald Reagan. In Dole's memorandum, she explains that the purpose of the meeting is 'to initiate your campaign to show small business that it has a true friend in the White House' (ibid.).

Kaiser's success in advocating for minority businesses was also noticed by her own clients. In 1984, she received a letter from Humphrey Sullivan, a public affairs director for Lever Brothers. Noting that her 21 years of service for the company was 'deeply appreciated', he commended her service on behalf of the Black business community.

"Probably more than most, I know how you have used that great vitality of yours not only to manage your business and raise your family but to fulfil the many commitments you have been asked to undertake over the years by several Administrations and organizations concerned with the issue of equal opportunity ... I look forward to seeing you at the Urban League meeting in Cleveland ..." (Sullivan 1984).

In 1987, when Kaiser was 69 years old, she opened a second business, called Pioneer Awards and Advertising Specialty Company. It sold a variety of promotional items for companies, African-American organizations, as well as for the Missouri Tourism Department. According to her son, Rick Kaiser, 'She literally was working on this until she died' (Kaiser 2020).

In a 1998 speech presented at City Hall in Kansas City in honour of Black History Month, Kaiser reviewed her achievements, struggles and dreams for future generations. She said she was proud she had taken the risk to open Inez Kaiser & Associates and that she helped change the bylaws of the Chamber of Commerce to read from 'White males only' to 'all business persons'. She went on to say that she was empowered to break down racial discrimination in business rental properties; and that her 'voice was raised repeatedly to speak out against injustice' (Kaiser 1998).

She had spent her life as an African-American businesswoman helping direct the paths of young people. She encouraged and supported many along their own paths and who, perhaps, had forgotten how they got there when they reached a higher plateau. She also had to build a bridge for young women to cross over into the world of business.

Conclusion

Inez Kaiser might not have made the leap from teaching to public relations had she not lost both of her parents early on in her life; her mother died when Inez was 11, and her father died when she was still a young school teacher. 'I had to work in order to survive', she wrote. 'No one was going to give me anything' (Kaiser Capabilities Statements). Shortly after her father's death and following an operation that kept her home from her teaching job, she had the time to think, reflect, read, pray and decide what she wanted to do with her life. Thanks to Howard Wood's suggestion that she should go into public relations, as well as feeling mistreated at her teaching job and subscribing to Napoleon Hill's philosophy that 'whatever the mind believes and conceives it can achieve', she was determined to go into business for herself (Kaiser 1998).

The year Kaiser started her agency was the same year two White men lynched 14-year-old Emmett Till, and Rosa Parks refused to relinquish her bus seat to a White passenger. It was also the same year nine Black students were prevented from entering their high school in Little Rock, Arkansas, and President Eisenhower signed the 1957 Civil Rights Act. Kaiser faced obstacles not just as a woman but also as a *Black* woman. She later noted that 'Kansas City is not the best city in the world to be an African-American and be in business' (Kaiser 2015). Despite the challenges she faced, she persisted. Not only was she the first African-American woman to open a public relations agency serving national accounts, she was also the first African-American woman to work with officials in Washington to advocate for women, especially minorities, to enter and succeed inside the business world (Kaiser 'Pioneering Efforts of Inez Kaiser' Backgrounder n.d.).

Inez Kaiser founded and ran a successful public relations agency, as well as an advertising specialty company, working until her death aged 98. She was a public relations pioneer, who rightfully deserves a place along the 'great White men'. In one of her last speeches, when she was in her early nineties, she said her prayer was that when her last project on earth was finished, someone would say, 'Inez Kaiser led the path for African-Americans in the business world and was a living example of an "Impossible Dream"' (Kaiser 1998).

'I have had my share of being ignored', Kaiser remarked. 'I kept on moving; I didn't let anyone stop me' (Kaiser 2015).

References

Berthiaune, D. (2013). 'Survey: Moms Still Make Most of the Household Purchase Decisions', *Chain Store Age*, [online] 24 October. Available at: https://chainstoreage.com/news/survey-moms-still-make-most-household-purchase-decisions (Accessed: 3 May 2020).

Broom, G. M. and Sha, B. -L. (2013) *Cutlip and Center's Effective Public Relations* (11th edn). Boston: Pearson.

Brunner, B. (2006). Where are the women? A content analysis of introductory public relations textbooks. *Public Relations Quarterly*, 51(3), 43–47.

Creedon, P. J. (1989). Public relations history misses 'her story'. *The Journalism Educator*, 44(3), 26–30.

Creedon, P. J. (2004). From making PR macho to making PR feminist, the battle over battles in a female-dominated field. In Ramona R. Rush, Carol E. Oukrop, and Pamela J. Creedon (Eds.), *Seeking Equity for Women in Journalism and Mass Communication Education: A 30-year Update*, (p. 224). London: Lawrence Erlbaum Associates.

Creedon, P. J. (2013). From making PR Macho to making PR feminist: The battle over values in a female-dominated field. In Rush, R., Oukrop, C. E. and Creedon, P. J (eds.), *Seeking Equity for Women in Journalism and Mass Communication Education* (pp. 232–250). Boca Raton: Routledge.

Cutlip, S. M. (1994). *The Unseen Power: Public Relations, a History*. Hillsdale, NJ: Lawrence Erlbaum.

Davis, J. F. (2013). Realizing marketplace opportunity. *Journal of Historical Research in Marketing*, 5(4), 471–493.

Dole, E. (1981). 'Leaders from the Small Business Community' Memorandum. Held at: New York: The Museum of Public Relations, Inez Kaiser Papers.

Fisher, Melody T. (2018). 'Respecting all Contributions: An Analysis of Inclusion in Public Relations Textbooks', *International History of Public Relations Conference*, Bournemouth, England, 11–12 July.

Gerz, W. (1964). Letter to Inez Kaiser. 20 November. Held at: New York: The Museum of Public Relations. Inez Kaiser Papers.

Gower, K. K. (2017). The historiography of North American public relations. In T. Watson (Ed.), *North American Perspectives on the Development of Public Relations: Other Voices*, (pp. 113–126). London: Palgrave MacMillan.

Hannon, S. W. (1997). *Almost Ten Years Later: An Analysis of Ethnic Inclusion in Public Relations Textbooks and Reference Books for the Years 1991–1997 as Compared to Kern-Foxworth's Analysis of Books for the Years 1979–1988.* Washington, DC: U.S. Department of Education, Educational Resources Information Center.

Henry, S. (1997). Anonymous in her own name: Public relations pioneer Doris E. Fleischman. *Journalism History*, 23(2), 51–62.

Henry, S. (1998). Dissonant notes of a retiring feminist: Doris E. Fleischman's later years. *Journal of Public Relations Research*, 10(1), 1–33.

Henry, S. (1999). 'There is nothing in this profession ... that a woman cannot do': Doris E. Fleischman and the beginnings of public relations. *American Journalism*, 16(2), 85–111.

Horsley, J.S. (2009). Women's contributions to American public relations, 1940–1970. *Journal of Communication Management*, 13(2), 100–115.

Kaiser, I. Y. (1968). *Soul Food Cookery* (3rd edn). New York: Pitman Publishing Corporation.

Kaiser, I. (1998). *African Americans in Business: The Path Toward Empowerment.* 24 February, City Hall, Kansas City, Mo.

Kaiser, I. (2015). Interviewed by Chelsea LeMar for The Museum of Public Relations. 19 February. Available at: www.prmuseum.org/video-and-audio?rq=inez%20kaiser (Accessed: 2 May 2020).

Kaiser, R. (2020). Correspondence with Shelley Spector. 22 May.

Kaiser, I. Capabilities Statements, n.d. Held at: New York: The Museum of Public Relations, Inez Kaiser Papers.

Kaiser, I. Company Background Promotional Flyer, n.d. Held at: New York: The Museum of Public Relations, Inez Kaiser Papers.

Kaiser, I. 'Inez Kaiser, Fashionwise and Otherwise', Promotional Flyer, n.d., Held at: New York: The Museum of Public Relations, Inez Kaiser Papers.

Kaiser, I. 'Personal Background', Promotional Flyer. n.d. Held at: New York: The Museum of Public Relations. Inez Kaiser Papers.

Kaiser, I. 'Pioneering Efforts of Inez Kaiser', Promotional Flyer, n.d. Held at: New York: The Museum of Public Relations, Inez Kaiser Papers.

Kaiser, I. 'Step into the Profitable Negro Market', Promotional Flyer. n.d. Held at: New York The Museum of Public Relations. Inez Kaiser Papers.

Keysor, C. F. (1953). 'The $15 Billion Negro Market', *Commerce*, September 1953, pp. 15, 46, 48–50.

Kern-Foxworth, M. (1989). Public relations books fail to show women in context. *The Journalism Educator*, 44(3), 31–36.

Kern-Foxworth, M. (1990). Ethnic inclusiveness in public relations textbooks and reference books. *Howard Journal of Communications*, 2(2), 226–237.

Lamme, M. O. (2001). Furious desires and victorious careers: Doris E. Fleischman, counsel on public relations and advocate for working women. *American Journalism*, 18(3), 13–33.

Lamme, M. O. (2007). Outside the prickly nest: Revisiting Doris Fleischman. *American Journalism*, 24(3), 85–107.

Liberman, S. (2011). *American Food by the Decades.* Santa Barbara: Greenwood.

Loken, B. (1968). Letter to Inez Kaiser. 23 April. Held at: New York: The Museum of Public Relations. Inez Kaiser Papers.

Martinelli, D. and Toth, E. (2010). Lessons on the big idea and public relations: Reflections on the 50-year career of Charlotte Klein. *Public Relations Journal*, 4(1). https://prjournal.instituteforpr.org/wp-content/uploads/Lessons-on-the-Big-Idea.pdf. (Accessed: 2 May 2020).

Miller, Karen S. (1997). Woman, man, lady, horse: Jane Stewart, public relations executive. *Public Relations Review*, 23(3), 249–269.

Page, J. T. and Parnell, L. J. (2019). *Introduction to Strategic Public Relations: Digital, Global, and Socially Responsible Communication*. Thousand Oaks, California: Sage Publications.

Patrick, N. (2010). 'Times Have Changed', *The Morning Sun*, 6 March. www.morningsun.net/article/20100306/NEWS/303069974. (Accessed: 1 May 2020).

Rodríguez-Salcedo, N. and Gómez-Baceiredo, B. (2017). A herstory of public relations: Teresa Dorn, from Scott Cutlip to Burson-Marsteller Europe (1974–1995). *Journal of Public Relations Research*, 29(1), 16–37.

Straughan, D. M. (2007). *Women's Use of Public Relations for Progressive-Era Reform: Rousing the Conscience of a Nation*. Lewiston: Edwin Mellen Press.

Sullivan, D. J. (1945). 'Negro Incomes and How They are Spent', reprint from 'How Negroes spent their incomes, 1920–1943', *Sales Management*, 15 June. Held at: Chicago: Chicago History Museum. Claude A. Barnett papers. Box 131.

Sullivan, H. (1984). Letter to Inez Kaiser. 20 June. Held at: New York: The Museum of Public Relations. Inez Kaiser Papers.

Today Show photograph. (1968). Held at: New York: The Museum of Public Relations. Inez Kaiser Papers.

Vardeman-Winter, J. and Place, K. R. (2017). Still a lily-white field of women: The state of workforce diversity in public relations practice and research. *Public Relations Review*, 43(2), 326–336.

Ward-Johnson, F. (2006). Public Relations as Social Activism: Ida B. Wells-Barnett and America's First Anti-Lynching Campaign, 10th International Public Relations Research Conference, 8–11 March.

White House Invitation-Inauguration of Richard Milhous Nixon and Spiro Theodore Agnew. (1972). Held at: New York: The Museum of Public Relations, Inez Kaiser Papers.

'The Negro Market: A fertile field for advertisers'. (1952), *Tide*, 24 July, pp. 43–49.

Conclusions

Anastasios Theofilou

The findings of this book are extremely insightful and allow us to draw some very useful conclusions. That being said, there should be an understanding that this is a first attempt to tell the 'her-story' in public relations; therefore, this book is merely the beginning of a journey to explore an exciting research area. There has been only scarce reference to how women have shaped the communication and public relations industry, even though their role historically can be traced back centuries. As Sthapitanonda indicates, while exploring Nang Noppamas in more of a proto-PR-like observation, women have been influencing, intentionally or not, PR-like activities.

Some interesting concluding points are made when looking into the era following PR professionalisation; women in PR have come a long way. As Donald Wright indicates, things may have improved from the time of the 'velvet ghetto' and 'glass ceiling'; however, his findings agree with Topić and Tench who report that despite progress, more challenges and different issues appear. Probably, consistent with other fields, women in PR still experience workplace discrimination, bias and prejudices (Topić et al., 2019), in addition to a pay gap. As Wright suggests, women in PR have come a long way; however, they still have a long way to go.

Another set of conclusions comes when exploring specific cases from different countries. By doing so, one may observe how women have been affecting the PR industry and education, as a whole, at national and international levels. For example, Aktas et al. indicate in their focus of the late 1960s when demand for public relations was evident, women excelled in the field and not only entered PR over the years but also achieved rather prestigious positions in international and national organisations. These findings agree with Hürmeriç and Bıçakçı who report how three Turkish women pioneers (Betûl Mardin, Ceyda Aydede and Zehra Güngör), who served as International Public Relations Association (IPRA) presidents in the decades 1990, 2000 and 2010, influenced the shape of the role performed by PR practitioners, a code of conduct and, of course, highlighted gender differences. Souket presents another excellent case when describing how Paddy Shubert made a breakthrough for women in PR education and the PR industry in Malaysia. Shubert seemed to have an extremely, perhaps intuitive, understanding for culture and led the way for women in both industries, that is, education and PR. Finally, another contribution from *national her-stories* is offered by Spencer and Hill who present the case of the first African-American pioneer of the field. The chapter, which is one of the first ever to focus on African-American pioneers, describes the inspiring story of Inez Kaiser who overcame race and gender-related obstacles. Kaiser's work influenced not only the PR industry but also gender and race equality. Inez Kaizer was the first woman to open a PR agency dealing with national accounts of her work advocating for women and minorities in the business world.

Women have also been affecting explicitly the development of the sector in niche areas like entertainment and arts, allowing us to draw some interesting concluding remarks. Fitch adds knowledge to this area when discussing how Stewart's work in entertainment PR offered a different angle beyond corporate parameters and from a gender perspective by going into PR in relation to lifestyle, sport, travel and retail, among other sectors. Stewart's campaign to promote *Oriental Cavalcade* produced and perpetuated stereotypes around Asian cultures. Stewart's work feminised and fetishised Asian women, as can be seen in Stewart's emphasis on beauty and national dress in communications prepared for the media. On a similar note, Guardia, Martínez and Xifra also found that arts and entertainment offered space for women PR pioneers to excel. In their work, they conclude how *Helena Lumbreras' filmography sheds light on the dual task of women in a private, domestic sphere when that sphere is turned into a space for struggle and intervention, while they also seek to maintain their place in the working world.*

In closing, one may observe that women historically have been affecting the field of PR from the times of proto-PR until recent times. Either through nature or nurture, women have excelled in contributing to all areas of PR at national and international levels, leaving a mark, laying foundations and, of course, contributing/leading developments.

As the editor of this book it has been fascinating reading and putting together all this historical data of women in PR. As stated above and as conclusions may indicate, this book is merely the beginning of something bigger. Exploring the role of women in PR is a work that may never be completed; however, this book has given it a heart to begin with. I cannot over-emphasise my thanks to colleagues who have contributed to this book, with my special thanks to a great friend, colleague and mentor, Prof. Tom Watson. Without Tom, this and many other projects would not have found the space to create the necessary knowledge for our discipline.

Index

activism 67, 70
activist 4, 5
activist public relations 67, 76
advertising 34–6
African-American practitioners 104
African-American women 6
Aktaş, Melike 2
American Women in Public Relations 9
Ankara 31, 32, 34, 35
Arthur W. Page Society 2
Asia Association of Management Organizations (AAMO) 86, 88
Australian Performing Arts Collection 57, 64
Australian public relations history 57, 63

Betty Stewart Collection 57, 60
Bıçakçı, Banu A. 3
Black tenants 107
British Malaya 81, 82
Buddhist 94–7

Canadian Public Relations Society 43
Civil Rights Act 112
Code of Ethics 46
Communication Consultancies Association of Turkey 39
communications industries 21–3, 25, 26
consultant 57, 59
cross promotion 61, 64
cultural historian 98
culture 83, 87, 89

decision-making 43, 49, 52, 53
dialogical approach 93
dissent public relations 67
documentaries 68, 75, 76, 87

ECM surveys 20–3, 25
educator 85, 89

entertainment public relations 57
equal opportunities 2
ethics codes 45, 46
European Communications Monitor 2, 18, 20
European Confederation of Public Relations (CERP) 41

female public relations managers 2
femininity 99, 102, 103
feminisation 19
feminised 62–4
fetishised 63
Fitch, Kate 3
Franco 4
Francoist regime 68
fundraising events 61

gender 21, 22, 24
gender differences 11, 14
gender diversity 1
gendered documentary 68
gender research 1, 9, 10, 12
glass ceiling 1, 9, 14, 15, 18–20, 22–6, 116
Global Alliance for Public Relations and Communication Management 43
Guardia, Isadora 4

Helena Lumbreras 4, 5, 67–71, 74–6, 117
herstories 4, 31, 64, 80, 89
heterosexual 106
Hill, Denise 6
Hill & Knowlton 106
Hindu 94, 95
Hindu tradition 95
history interview 58, 60
Hürmeriç, Pelin 3

IABC Foundation 1, 9
"ideal" woman 6

Index 119

inequality 21, 26
Institute of Public Relations Malaysia (IPRM) 5, 43, 46, 84–6, 88
International Association of Business Communicators (IABC) 41
International History of Public Relations Conference (IHPRC) 1
internationalization of public relations 31
International Public Relations Association (IPRA) 2, 3, 33, 34, 36, 41
IPRA presidents 42, 49, 53, 54
issues management 67
Italian Communist Party 4

job dissatisfaction 2
job satisfaction 2
journalism's culture 18

Kaiser, Inez 6, 104, 106–8, 112, 113
King Ramkhamhaeng 94

Loi Krathong Festival 5, 91, 94–9, 102
lunar calendar 95, 101

Malaysian public relations 5, 80, 81, 84, 89
Mardin, Betül 33–7, 41, 42, 44, 46, 48–53
Martínez, Carolina 4
Marxist 74
media relations 4
memoir 81–3, 89
mentors 35, 36
'militant' 67, 69
Ms. Noppamas 5

Nang Noppamas 91, 92, 94–103
narratives 37
National Association of Minority Women in Business 111
National Urban League 107, 110
North American public relations 105

Oriental Cavalcade 3, 57–9, 117
orientalism 57, 62
O todos o ninguno 4
Özdemir, Pınar 2

Paddy: A Lifetime of Memories 5
pay gap 2, 18–20, 22–4, 26, 116
pioneering woman 32
political crisis 87
political sciences 32
popular culture 20
PR consultancy 87
PR education 2, 10, 116

presidents of IPRA 41, 43, 46
PR industry in Malaysia 116
prism 41
PR-like activities 116
PR professionals 42, 48, 91, 92
professionalization 31, 33
professional narrative 64
professional standards 41–3, 48, 53, 54
professional training 48
professional women 31
protest public relations 67
PR Week 10
Public Relations Association of Turkey 2
Public Relations Company 57, 59
public relations in Australia 4
public relations industry 1, 9–12, 14
public relations pioneer 113
public relations profession 41, 42, 46, 49, 51, 52
public relations scholars 19
Public Relations Society of America (PRSA) 9, 41
'public thinking' 93

race 83, 89
racial equity 43, 50
RAI 4
Royal family 94, 96

salary differences 11, 15
Schubert, Paddy 5, 80–2, 84–9
'Signum authenticum' 31
situational constraints 43, 51
social responsibilities 49
sponsorship 61
Stewart, Betty 4, 57, 58, 60, 62
Sthapitanonda, Parichart 5
strategic planning 43, 52

teaching public relations 37
technician roles 24
Thai culture 91, 94, 96, 100, 101
Thai female PR practitioner 91, 92, 101
Thailand 91, 94, 96, 99, 100
Thai oral history 96, 97
thematic analysis 18, 22
Tivoli 57–61
Topić, Martina 2
Tourism Authority 99
Turkey 31–4, 36
Turkish PR history 42
Turkish women 41, 42, 53, 54
Turkish women pioneers 116

US public relations history 104, 105

"velvet ghetto" 1, 9, 10, 14, 15, 116
visual communications 26
voice of the women 73

Watson, Tom 117
women in public relations 18–21, 24, 26
Women in Public Relations Leadership 11

women PR pioneer 80
women PR practitioners 41, 51
Women's Christian Temperance Union 106
work environment 23–6
Wright, Donald 1

Xifra, Jordi 4

Printed in the United States
By Bookmasters